Sigrid Estrada

Barbara Ehrenreich is the bestselling author of sixteen previous books, including the bestsellers *Bright-Sided* and *Bait and Switch*. A frequent contributor to *Harper's* and *The Nation,* she has also been a columnist at *The New York Times* and *Time* magazine.

Also by Barbara Ehrenreich

This Land Is Their Land: Reports from a Divided Nation

Bait and Switch: The (Futile) Pursuit of the American Dream

Dancing in the Streets: A History of Collective Joy

Blood Rites: Origins and History of the Passions of War

The Snarling Citizen

Kipper's Game

The Worst Years of Our Lives: Irreverent Notes from a Decade of Greed

Fear of Falling: The Inner Life of the Middle Class

The Hearts of Men: American Dreams and the Flight from Commitment

Global Woman: Nannies, Maids, and Sex Workers in the New Economy
(with Arlie Russell Hochschild)

Re-Making Love: The Feminization of Sex
(with Elizabeth Hess and Gloria Jacobs)

For Her Own Good: Two Centuries of the Experts' Advice to Women
(with Deirdre English)

Witches, Midwives, and Nurses: A History of Women Healers
(with Deirdre English)

Complaints and Disorders: The Sexual Politics of Sickness
(with Deirdre English)

The Mean Season: The Attack on the Welfare State
(with Fred Block, Richard A. Cloward, and Frances Fox Piven)

Bright-Sided: How Positive Thinking Is Undermining America

Additional Praise for
Nickel and Dimed: On (Not) Getting By in America

"Eloquent . . . This book illuminates the invisible army that scrubs floors, waits tables, and straightens the racks at discount stores." —Sandy Block, *USA Today*

"Courageous . . . *Nickel and Dimed* is a superb and frightening look into the lives of hard-working Americans. . . . Policy makers should be forced to read it."
—Tamara Straus, *San Francisco Chronicle*

"I was absolutely knocked out by Barbara Ehrenreich's remarkable odyssey. She has accomplished what no contemporary writer has ever attempted—to be that 'nobody' who barely subsists on her essential labors. *Nickel and Dimed* is a stiff punch in the nose to righteous apostles of 'welfare reform.' Not only is it must-reading, but it's mesmeric. You can't put the damn thing down. Bravo!"
—Studs Terkel, author of *Working*

"*Nickel and Dimed* opens a window into the daily lives of the invisible workforce that fuels the service economy, and endows the men and women who populate it with the honor that is often lacking on the job. And it forces the reader to realize that all the good-news talk about welfare reform masks a harsher reality."
—Katherine Newman, *The Washington Post*

"With grace and wit, Ehrenreich discovers the irony of being 'nickel and dimed' during unprecedented prosperity. . . . Living wages, she elegantly shows, might erase the shame that comes from our dependence 'on the underpaid labor of others.'" —Eileen Boris, *The Boston Globe*

"It is not difficult to endorse *Nickel and Dimed* as a book that everyone who reads—yes, everyone—ought to read for enjoyment, for consciousness-raising, and as a call to action." —Steve Weinberg, *Chicago Tribune*

"Unflinching, superb . . . *Nickel and Dimed* is an important book that should be read by anyone who has been lulled into middle-class complacency." —Vivien Labaton, *Ms.* magazine

"Brief but intense . . . *Nickel and Dimed* is an accessible yet relentless look at the lives of the American underclass." —David Ulin, *Los Angeles Times*

"Observant, opinionated, and always lively . . . What makes *Nickel and Dimed* such an important book is how viscerally Ehrenreich demonstrates that the method of calculating the poverty threshold is ludicrously obsolete." —Laura Miller, *Salon*

"One of the great American social critics has written an unforgettable memoir of what it was like to work in some of America's least attractive jobs. No one who reads this book will be able to resist its power to make them see the world in a new way." —Mitchell Duneier, author of *Sidewalk*

"In *Nickel and Dimed,* Ehrenreich expertly peels away the layers of self-denial, self-interest, and self-protection that separate the rich from the poor, the served from the servers, the housed from the homeless. This brave and frank book is ultimately a challenge to create a less divided society."
—Naomi Klein, author of *No Logo* and *The Shock Doctrine*

"Piercing social criticism backed by first-rate reporting . . . Ehrenreich captures not only the tribulations of finding and performing low-wage work, but the humiliations as well."
—Eric Wieffering, *Minneapolis Star Tribune*

"Engaging . . . Hopefully, *Nickel and Dimed* will expand public awareness of the real-world survival struggles that many faced even before the current economic downturn."
—Steve Early, *The Nation*

"Entering the world of service work, Barbara Ehrenreich folded clothes at Wal-Mart, waitressed, washed dishes in a nursing home, and scrubbed floors on her hands and knees. Her account of those experiences is unforgettable— heart-wrenching, infuriating, funny, smart, and empowering. Few readers will be untouched by the shameful realities that underlie America's economy. Vintage Ehrenreich, *Nickel and Dimed* will surely take its place among the classics of underground reportage."
—Juliet Schor, author of *The Overworked American*

Nickel

and

Dimed

ON (NOT) GETTING
BY IN AMERICA

Barbara Ehrenreich

Picador

A Metropolitan Book
Henry Holt and Company
New York

www.picadorusa.com

Picador® is a U.S. registered trademark and is used by Henry Holt and Company under license from Pan Books Limited.

For information on Picador Reading Group Guides, please contact Picador.
E-mail: readinggroupguides@picadorusa.com

Designed by Kelly S. Too

Library of Congress Cataloging-in-Publication Data

Ehrenreich, Barbara.
    Nickel and dimed : on (not) getting by in America / Barbara Ehrenreich. — 1st Picador ed.
      p. cm.
    ISBN 978-0-312-62668-6 (pbk.)
    1. Minimum wage—United States. 2. Working poor—United States. 3. Unskilled labor—United States. 4. Poverty—United States. I. Title.
    HD4918.E375 2011
    305.5'69092—dc22
    [B]

2011013114

First published in the United States by Metropolitan Books, an imprint of Henry Holt and Company

First Picador Edition: August 2011

10   9   8

contents

Nickel and Dimed

Introduction: Getting Ready

The idea that led to this book arose in comparatively sumptuous circumstances. Lewis Lapham, the editor of *Harper's,* had taken me out for a $30 lunch at some understated French country-style place to discuss future articles I might write for his magazine. I had the salmon and field greens, I think, and was pitching him some ideas having to do with pop culture when the conversation drifted to one of my more familiar themes—poverty. How does anyone live on the wages available to the unskilled? How, in particular, we wondered, were the roughly four million women about to be booted into the labor market by welfare reform going to make it on $6 or $7 an hour? Then I said something that I have since had many opportunities to regret: "Someone ought to do the old-fashioned kind of journalism—you know, go out there and try it for themselves." I meant someone much younger than myself, some hungry neophyte journalist with time on her hands. But Lapham got this crazy-looking half smile on his face and ended life as I knew it, for long stretches at least, with the single word *"You."*

The last time anyone had urged me to forsake my normal life for a run-of-the-mill low-paid job had been in the seventies, when dozens, perhaps hundreds, of sixties radicals started going into the factories to "proletarianize" themselves and organize the working class in the process. Not this girl. I felt sorry for the parents who had paid college tuition for these blue-collar wannabes and sorry, too, for the people they intended to uplift. In my own family, the low-wage way of life had never been many degrees of separation away; it was close enough, in any case, to make me treasure the gloriously autonomous, if not always well-paid, writing life. My sister has been through one low-paid job after another—phone company business rep, factory worker, receptionist—constantly struggling against what she calls "the hopelessness of being a wage slave." My husband and companion of seventeen years was a $4.50-an-hour warehouse worker when I fell in with him, escaping eventually and with huge relief to become an organizer for the Teamsters. My father had been a copper miner; uncles and grandfathers worked in the mines or for the Union Pacific. So to me, sitting at a desk all day was not only a privilege but a duty: something I owed to all those people in my life, living and dead, who'd had so much more to say than anyone ever got to hear.

Adding to my misgivings, certain family members kept reminding me unhelpfully that I could do this project, after a fashion, without ever leaving my study. I could just pay myself a typical entry-level wage for eight hours a day, charge myself for room and board plus some plausible expenses like gas, and total up the numbers after a month. With the prevailing wages running at $6–$7 an hour in my town and rents at $400 a month or more, the numbers might, it seemed to me, just barely work out all right. But if the question was whether a single mother leaving welfare could survive without government assistance in the form of food stamps, Medicaid, and housing and child care subsidies, the answer was well known before I ever left the comforts of home. According to the National Coalition for the Homeless, in 1998—the year I started this project—it took, on average nationwide, an hourly wage of $8.89 to afford a one-bedroom apartment, and the Preamble Center for Public Policy was estimating that the odds against a typical welfare recipient's landing a job at such a "living wage" were about 97 to 1. Why should I bother to confirm these unpleasant facts? As the time when I could no longer avoid the assignment approached, I began to feel a little like the elderly man I once knew who used a calculator to balance his checkbook and then went back and checked the results by redoing each sum by hand.

In the end, the only way to overcome my hesitation was by thinking of myself as a scientist, which is, in fact, what I was educated to be. I have a Ph.D. in biology, and I didn't get it by sitting at a desk and fiddling with numbers. In that line of business, you can think all you want, but sooner or later you have to get to the bench and plunge into the everyday chaos of nature, where surprises lurk in the most mundane measurements. Maybe when I got into the project, I would discover some hidden economies in the world of the low-wage worker. After all, if almost 30 percent of the workforce toils for $8 an hour or less, as the Washington-based Economic Policy Institute reported in 1998, they may have found some tricks as yet unknown to me. Maybe I would even be able to detect in myself the bracing psychological effects of getting out of the house, as promised by the wonks who brought us welfare reform. Or, on the other hand, maybe there would be unexpected costs—physical, financial, emotional—to throw off all my calculations. The only way to find out was to get out there and get my hands dirty.

In the spirit of science, I first decided on certain rules and parameters. Rule one, obviously enough, was that I could not, in my search for jobs, fall back on any skills derived from my education or usual work—not that there were a lot of want ads for essayists anyway. Two, I had to take the highest-paying job that was offered me and do my best to hold it; no Marxist rants or sneaking off to read novels in the ladies' room. Three, I had to take the cheapest accommodations I could find, at least the cheapest that offered an acceptable level of safety and privacy, though my standards in this regard were hazy and, as it turned out, prone to deterioration over time.

I tried to stick to these rules, but in the course of the project, all of them were bent or broken at some time. In Key West, for example, where I began this project in the late spring of 1998, I once promoted myself to an interviewer for a waitressing job by telling her I could greet European tourists with the appropriate *Bonjour* or *Guten Tag,* but this was the only case in which I drew on any remnant of my actual education. In Minneapolis, my final destination, where I lived in the early summer of 2000, I broke another rule by failing to take the best-paying job that was offered, and you will have to judge my reasons for doing so yourself. And finally, toward the very end, I did break down and rant—stealthily, though, and never within hearing of management.

There was also the problem of how to present myself to potential employers and, in particular, how to explain my dismal lack of relevant job experience. The truth, or at least a drastically stripped-down version thereof, seemed easiest: I described myself to interviewers as a divorced homemaker reentering the workforce after many years, which is true as far as it goes. Sometimes, though not always, I would throw in a few housecleaning jobs, citing as references former housemates and a friend in Key West whom I have at least helped with after-dinner cleanups now and then. Job application forms also want to know about education, and here I figured the Ph.D. would be no help at all, might even lead employers to suspect that I was an alcoholic washout or worse. So I confined myself to three years of college, listing my real-life alma mater. No one ever questioned my background, as it turned out, and only one employer out of several dozen bothered to check my references. When, on one occasion, an exceptionally chatty interviewer asked about hobbies, I said "writing" and she seemed to find nothing strange about this, although the job she was offering could have been performed perfectly well by an illiterate.

Finally, I set some reassuring limits to whatever tribulations I might have to endure. First, I would always have a car. In Key West I drove my own; in other cities I used Rent-A-Wrecks, which I paid for with a credit card rather than my earnings. Yes, I could have walked more or limited myself to jobs accessible by public transportation. I just figured that a story about waiting for buses would not be very interesting to read. Second, I ruled out homelessness as an option. The idea was to spend a month in each setting and see whether I could find a job and earn, in that time, the money to pay a second month's rent. If I was paying rent by the week and ran out of money I would simply declare the project at an end; no shelters or sleeping in cars for me. Furthermore, I had no intention of going hungry. If things ever got to the point where the next meal was in question, I promised myself as the time to begin the "experiment" approached, I would dig out my ATM card and cheat.

So this is not a story of some death-defying "undercover" adventure. Almost anyone could do what I did—look for jobs, work those jobs, try to make ends meet. In fact, millions of Americans do it every day, and with a lot less fanfare and dithering.

I AM, OF COURSE, VERY DIFFERENT FROM THE PEOPLE WHO NORMALLY fill America's least attractive jobs, and in ways that both helped and limited me. Most obviously, I was only visiting a world that others inhabit full-time, often for most of their lives. With all the real-life assets I've built up in middle age—bank account, IRA, health insurance, multiroom home—waiting indulgently in the background, there was no way I was going to "experience poverty" or find out how it "really feels" to be a long-term low-wage worker. My aim here was much more straightforward and objective—just to see whether I could match income to expenses, as the truly poor attempt to do every day. Besides, I've had enough unchosen encounters with poverty in my lifetime to know it's not a place you would want to visit for touristic purposes; it just smells too much like fear.

Unlike many low-wage workers, I have the further advantages of being white and a native English speaker. I don't think this affected my chances of getting a job, given the willingness of employers to hire almost anyone in the tight labor market of

1998 to 2000, but it almost certainly affected the *kinds* of jobs I was offered. In Key West, I originally sought what I assumed would be a relatively easy job in hotel housekeeping and found myself steered instead into waitressing, no doubt because of my ethnicity and my English skills. As it happened, waitressing didn't provide much of a financial advantage over house-keeping, at least not in the low-tip off-season when I worked in Key West. But the experience did help determine my choice of other localities in which to live and work. I ruled out places like New York and L.A., for example, where the working class consists mainly of people of color and a white woman with unaccented English seeking entry-level jobs might only look desperate or weird.

I had other advantages—the car, for example—that set me off from many, though hardly all, of my coworkers. Ideally, at least if I were seeking to replicate the experience of a woman entering the workforce from welfare, I would have had a couple of children in tow, but mine are grown and no one was willing to lend me theirs for a monthlong vacation in penury. In addi-tion to being mobile and unencumbered, I am probably in a lot better health than most members of the long-term low-wage workforce. I had everything going for me.

If there were other, subtler things different about me, no one ever pointed them out. Certainly I made no effort to play a role or fit into some imaginative stereotype of low-wage work-ing women. I wore my usual clothes, wherever ordinary clothes were permitted, and my usual hairstyle and makeup. In con-versations with coworkers, I talked about my real children, marital status, and relationships; there was no reason to invent a whole new life. I did modify my vocabulary, however, in one respect: at least when I was new at a job and worried about seeming brash or disrespectful, I censored the profanities that are—thanks largely to the Teamster influence—part of my normal speech. Other than that, I joked and teased, offered opinions, speculations, and, incidentally, a great deal of health-related advice, exactly as I would do in any other setting.

Several times since completing this project I have been asked by acquaintances whether the people I worked with couldn't, uh, *tell*—the supposition being that an educated person is ineradicably different, and in a superior direction, from your workaday drones. I wish I could say that some supervisor or coworker told me even once that I was special in some enviable way—more intelligent, for example, or clearly better educated than most. But this never happened, I suspect because the only thing that really made me "special" was my inexperience. To state the proposition in reverse, low-wage workers are no more homogeneous in personality or ability than people who write for a living, and no less likely to be funny or bright. Anyone in the educated classes who thinks otherwise ought to broaden their circle of friends.

There was always, of course, the difference that only I knew—that I wasn't working for the money, I was doing research for an article and later a book. I went home every day not to anything resembling a normal domestic life but to a laptop on which I spent an hour or two recording the day's events—very diligently, I should add, since note taking was seldom an option during the day. This deception, symbolized by the laptop that provided a link to my past and future, bothered me, at least in the case of people I cared about and wanted to know better. (I should mention here that names and identifying details have been altered to preserve the privacy of the people I worked with and encountered in other settings during the course of my research. In most cases, I have also changed the names of the places I worked and their exact locations to further ensure the anonymity of people I met.)

In each setting, toward the end of my stay and after much anxious forethought, I "came out" to a few chosen coworkers. The result was always stunningly anticlimactic, my favorite response being, "Does this mean you're not going to be back on the evening shift next week?" I've wondered a lot about why there wasn't more astonishment or even indignation, and part of the answer probably lies in people's notion of "writing." Years ago, when I married my second husband, he proudly told his uncle, who was a valet parker at the time, that I was a writer. The uncle's response: "Who isn't?" Everyone literate "writes," and some of the low-wage workers I have known or met through this project write journals and poems— even, in one case, a lengthy science fiction novel.

But as I realized very late in this project, it may also be that I was exaggerating the extent of the "deception" to myself. There's no way, for example, to pretend to be a waitress: the food either gets to the table or not. People knew me as a waitress, a cleaning person, a nursing home aide, or a retail clerk not because I acted like one but because that's what I *was,* at least for the time I was with them. In every job, in every place I lived, the work absorbed all my energy and much of my intellect. I wasn't kidding around. Even though I suspected from the start that the mathematics of wages and rents were working against me, I made a mighty effort to succeed.

I make no claims for the relevance of my experiences to anyone else's, because there is nothing typical about my story.

Just bear in mind, when I stumble, that this is in fact the *best*-case scenario: a person with every advantage that ethnicity and education, health and motivation can confer attempting, in a time of exuberant prosperity, to survive in the economy's lower depths.

one

Serving in Florida

Mostly out of laziness, I decide to start my low-wage life in the town nearest to where I actually live, Key West, Florida, which with a population of about 25,000 is elbowing its way up to the status of a genuine city. The downside of familiarity, I soon realize, is that it's not easy to go from being a consumer, thoughtlessly throwing money around in exchange for groceries and movies and gas, to being a worker in the very same place. I am terrified, especially at the beginning, of being recognized by some friendly business owner or erstwhile neighbor and having to stammer out some explanation of my project. Happily, though, my fears turn out to be entirely unwarranted: during a month of poverty and toil, no one recognizes my face or my name, which goes unnoticed and for the most part unuttered. In this parallel universe where my father never got out of the mines and I never got through college, I am "baby," "honey," "blondie," and, most commonly, "girl."

My first task is to find a place to live. I figure that if I can earn $7 an hour—which, from the want ads, seems doable— I can afford to spend $500 on rent or maybe, with severe economies, $600 and still have $400 or $500 left over for food and gas. In the Key West area, this pretty much confines me to flophouses and trailer homes—like the one, a pleasing fifteen-minute drive from town, that has no air-conditioning, no screens, no fans, no television, and, by way of diversion, only the challenge of evading the landlord's Doberman pinscher. The big problem with this place, though, is the rent, which at $675 a month is well beyond my reach. All right, Key West is expensive. But so is New York City, or the Bay Area, or Jackson, Wyoming, or Telluride, or Boston, or any other place where tourists and the wealthy compete for living space with the people who clean their toilets and fry their hash browns. Still, it is a shock to realize that "trailer trash" has become, for me, a demographic category to aspire to.

So I decide to make the common trade-off between afford-ability and convenience and go for a $500-a-month "efficiency" thirty miles up a two-lane highway from the employment opportunities of Key West, meaning forty-five minutes if there's no road construction and I don't get caught behind some sun-dazed Canadian tourists. I hate the drive, along a roadside studded with white crosses commemorating the more effective head-on collisions, but it's a sweet little place—a cabin, more or less, set in the swampy backyard of the converted mobile home where my landlord, an affable TV repairman, lives with his bartender girlfriend. Anthropologically speaking, the trailer park would be preferable, but here I have a gleaming white floor and a firm mattress, and the few resident bugs are easily vanquished.

The next piece of business is to comb through the want ads and find a job. I rule out various occupations for one reason or another: hotel front-desk clerk, for example, which to my surprise is regarded as unskilled and pays only $6 or $7 an hour, gets eliminated because it involves standing in one spot for eight hours a day. Waitressing is also something I'd like to avoid, because I remember it leaving me bone-tired when I was eighteen, and I'm decades of varicosities and back pain beyond that now. Telemarketing, one of the first refuges of the suddenly indigent, can be dismissed on grounds of personality. This leaves certain supermarket jobs, such as deli clerk, or housekeeping in the hotels and guest houses, which pays about $7 and, I imagine, is not too different from what I've been doing part-time, in my own home, all my life.

So I put on what I take to be a respectable-looking outfit of ironed Bermuda shorts and scooped-neck T-shirt and set out for a tour of the local hotels and supermarkets. Best Western, Econo Lodge, and HoJo's all let me fill out application forms, and these are, to my relief, mostly interested in whether I am a legal resident of the United States and have committed any felonies. My next stop is Winn-Dixie, the supermarket, which turns out to have a particularly onerous application process, featuring a twenty-minute "interview" by computer since, apparently, no human on the premises is deemed capable of representing the corporate point of view. I am conducted to a large room decorated with posters illustrating how to look "professional" (it helps to be white and, if female, permed) and warning of the slick promises that union organizers might try to tempt me with. The interview is multiple-choice: Do I have anything, such as child care problems, that might make it hard for me to get to work on time? Do I think safety on the job is the responsibility of management? Then, popping up cunningly out of the blue: How many dollars' worth of stolen goods have I purchased in the last year? Would I turn in a fellow employee if I caught him stealing? Finally, "Are you an honest person?"

Apparently I ace the interview, because I am told that all I have to do is show up in some doctor's office tomorrow for a urine test. This seems to be a fairly general rule: if you want to stack Cheerios boxes or vacuum hotel rooms in chemically fascist America, you have to be willing to squat down and pee in front of a health worker (who has no doubt had to do the same thing herself.)[1] The wages Winn-Dixie is offering—$6 and a couple of dimes to start with—are not enough, I decide, to compensate for this indignity.

I lunch at Wendy's, where $4.99 gets you unlimited refills at the Mexican part of the Super-bar, a comforting surfeit of refried beans and cheese sauce. A teenage employee, seeing me studying the want ads, kindly offers me an application form, which I fill out, though here, too, the pay is just $6 and change an hour. Then it's off for a round of the locally owned inns and guest houses in Key West's Old Town, which is where all the serious sightseeing and guzzling goes on, a couple of miles removed from the functional end of the island, where the dis-

---

[1] Eighty-one percent of large employers now require preemployment drug testing, up from 21 percent in 1987. Among all employers, the rate of testing is highest in the South. The drug most likely to be detected—marijuana, which can be detected weeks after use—is also the most innocuous, while heroin and cocaine are generally undetectable three days after use. Alcohol, which clears the body within hours after ingestion, is not tested for.

count hotels make their homes. At The Palms, let's call it, a bouncy manager actually takes me around to see the rooms and meet the current housekeepers, who, I note with satisfaction, look pretty much like me—faded ex-hippie types in shorts with long hair pulled back in braids. Mostly, though, no one speaks to me or even looks at me except to proffer an application form. At my last stop, a palatial B & B, I wait twenty minutes to meet "Max," only to be told that there are no jobs now but there should be one soon, since "nobody lasts more than a couple weeks."

Three days go by like this and, to my chagrin, no one from the approximately twenty places at which I've applied calls me for an interview. I had been vain enough to worry about coming across as too educated for the jobs I sought, but no one even seems interested in finding out how overqualified I am. Only later will I realize that the want ads are not a reliable measure of the actual jobs available at any particular time. They are, as I should have guessed from Max's comment, the employers' insurance policy against the relentless turnover of the low-wage workforce. Most of the big hotels run ads almost continually, if only to build a supply of applicants to replace the current workers as they drift away or are fired, so finding a job is just a matter of being in the right place at the right time and flexible enough to take whatever is being offered that day. This finally happens to me at one of the big discount chain hotels where I go, as usual, for housekeeping and am sent instead to try out as a waitress at the attached "family restaurant," a dismal spot looking out on a parking garage, which is featuring "Pollish sausage and BBQ sauce" on this 95-degree day. Phillip, the dapper young West Indian who introduces himself as the manager, interviews me with about as much enthusiasm as if he were a clerk processing me for Medicare, the principal questions being what shifts I can work and when I can start. I mutter about being woefully out of practice as a waitress, but he's already on to the uniform: I'm to show up tomorrow wearing black slacks and black shoes; he'll provide the rust-colored polo shirt with "Hearthside," as we'll call the place, embroidered on it, though I might want to wear my own shirt to get to work, ha ha. At the word *tomorrow,* something between fear and indignation rises in my chest. I want to say, "Thank you for your time, sir, but this is just an experiment, you know, not my actual life."

SO BEGINS MY CAREER AT THE HEARTHSIDE, WHERE FOR TWO WEEKS I work from 2:00 till 10:00 P.M. for $2.43 an hour plus tips.[2] Employees are barred from using the front door, so I enter the first day through the kitchen, where a red-faced man with shoulder-length blond hair is throwing frozen steaks against the wall and yelling, "Fuck this shit!" "That's just Billy," explains Gail, the wiry middle-aged waitress who is assigned to train me. "He's on the rag again"—a condition occasioned, in this instance, by the fact that the cook on the morning shift had forgotten to thaw out the steaks. For the next eight hours, I run after the agile Gail, absorbing bits of instruction along with fragments of personal tragedy. All food must be trayed, and the reason she's so tired today is that she woke up in a cold sweat thinking of her boyfriend, who was killed a few months ago in

---

[2] According to the Fair Labor Standards Act, employers are not required to pay "tipped employees," such as restaurant servers, more than $2.13 an hour in direct wages. However, if the sum of tips plus $2.13 an hour falls below the minimum wage, or $5.15 an hour, the employer is required to make up the difference. This fact was not mentioned by managers or otherwise publicized at either of the restaurants where I worked.

a scuffle in an upstate prison. No refills on lemonade. And the reason he was in prison is that a few DUIs caught up with him, that's all, could have happened to anyone. Carry the creamers to the table in a "monkey bowl," never in your hand. And after he was gone she spent several months living in her truck, peeing in a plastic pee bottle and reading by candlelight at night, but you can't live in a truck in the summer, since you need to have the windows down, which means anything can get in, from mosquitoes on up.

At least Gail puts to rest any fears I had of appearing overqualified. From the first day on, I find that of all the things that I have left behind, such as home and identity, what I miss the most is competence. Not that I have ever felt 100 percent competent in the writing business, where one day's success augurs nothing at all for the next. But in my writing life, I at least have some notion of *procedure:* do the research, make the outline, rough out a draft, etc. As a server, though, I am beset by requests as if by bees: more iced tea here, catsup over there, a to-go box for table 14, and where are the high chairs, anyway? Of the twenty-seven tables, up to six are usually mine at any time, though on slow afternoons or if Gail is off, I sometimes have the whole place to myself. There is the touch-screen computer-ordering system to master, which I suppose is meant to minimize server-cook contacts but in practice requires constant verbal fine-tuning: "That's gravy on the mashed, OK? None on the meatloaf," and so forth. Plus, something I had forgotten in the years since I was eighteen: about a third of a server's job is "side work" invisible to customers—sweeping, scrubbing, slicing, refilling, and restocking. If it isn't all done, every little bit of it, you're going to face the 6:00 P.M. dinner rush defenseless and probably go down in flames. I screw up dozens of times at the beginning, sustained in my shame entirely by Gail's support—"It's OK, baby, everyone does that sometime"—because, to my total surprise and despite the scientific detachment I am doing my best to maintain, I *care*.

The whole thing would be a lot easier if I could just skate through it like Lily Tomlin in one of her waitress skits, but I was raised by the absurd Booker T. Washingtonian precept that says: If you're going to do something, do it well. In fact, "well" isn't good enough by half. Do it better than anyone has ever done it before. Or so said my father, who must have known what he was talking about because he managed to pull himself, and us with him, up from the mile-deep copper mines of Butte to the leafy suburbs of the Northeast, ascending from boiler-makers to martinis before booze beat out ambition. As in most endeavors I have encountered in my life, "doing it better than anyone" is not a reasonable goal. Still, when I wake up at 4 A.M. in my own cold sweat, I am not thinking about the writing deadlines I'm neglecting; I'm thinking of the table where I screwed up the order and one of the kids didn't get his kiddie meal until the rest of the family had moved on to their Key lime pies. That's the other powerful motivation—the customers, or "patients," as I can't help thinking of them on account of the mysterious vulnerability that seems to have left them temporarily unable to feed themselves. After a few days at Hearth-side, I feel the service ethic kick in like a shot of oxytocin, the nurturance hormone. The plurality of my customers are hardworking locals—truck drivers, construction workers, even housekeepers from the attached hotel—and I want them to have the closest to a "fine dining" experience that the grubby circumstances will allow. No "you guys" for me; everyone over twelve is "sir" or "ma'am." I ply them with iced tea and coffee refills; I return, midmeal, to inquire how everything is; I doll up their salads with chopped raw mushrooms, summer squash slices, or whatever bits of produce I can find that have survived their sojourn in the cold storage room mold-free.

There is Benny, for example, a short, tight-muscled sewer repairman who cannot even think of eating until he has absorbed a half hour of air-conditioning and ice water. We chat about hyperthermia and electrolytes until he is ready to order some finicky combination like soup of the day, garden salad, and a side of grits. There are the German tourists who are so touched by my pidgin *"Wilkommen"* and *"Ist alles gut?"* that they actually tip. (Europeans, no doubt spoiled by their trade union–ridden, high-wage welfare states, generally do not know that they are supposed to tip. Some restaurants, the Hearthside included, allow servers to "grat" their foreign customers, or add a tip to the bill. Since this amount is added before the customers have a chance to tip or not tip, the practice amounts to an automatic penalty for imperfect English.) There are the two dirt-smudged lesbians, just off from their shift, who are impressed enough by my suave handling of the fly in the piña colada that they take the time to praise me to Stu, the assistant manager. There's Sam, the kindly retired cop who has to plug up his tracheotomy hole with one finger in order to force the cigarette smoke into his lungs.

Sometimes I play with the fantasy that I am a princess who, in penance for some tiny transgression, has undertaken to feed each of her subjects by hand. But the nonprincesses working with me are just as indulgent, even when this means flouting management rules—as to, for example, the number of croutons that can go on a salad (six). "Put on all you want," Gail whispers, "as long as Stu isn't looking." She dips into her own tip money to buy biscuits and gravy for an out-of-work mechanic who's used up all his money on dental surgery, inspiring me to pick up the tab for his pie and milk. Maybe the same high levels of agape can be found throughout the "hospitality industry." I remember the poster decorating one of the apartments I looked at, which said, "If you seek happiness for yourself you will never find it. Only when you seek happiness for others will it come to you," or words to that effect—an odd sentiment, it seemed to me at the time, to find in the dank one-room basement apartment of a bellhop at the Best Western. At Hearthside, we utilize whatever bits of autonomy we have to ply our customers with the illicit calories that signal our love. It is our job as servers to assemble the salads and desserts, pour the dressings, and squirt the whipped cream. We also control the number of butter pats our customers get and the amount of sour cream on their baked potatoes. So if you wonder why Americans are so obese, consider the fact that waitresses both express their humanity and earn their tips through the covert distribution of fats.

Ten days into it, this is beginning to look like a livable lifestyle. I like Gail, who is "looking at fifty," agewise, but moves so fast she can alight in one place and then another without apparently being anywhere between. I clown around with Lionel, the teenage Haitian busboy, though we don't have much vocabulary in common, and loiter near the main sink to listen to the older Haitian dishwashers' musical Creole, which sounds, in their rich bass voices, like French on testosterone. I bond with Timmy, the fourteen-year-old white kid who buses at night, by telling him I don't like people putting their baby seats right on the tables: it makes the baby look too much like a side dish. He snickers delightedly and in return, on a slow

night, starts telling me the plots of all the *Jaws* movies (which
are perennial favorites in the shark-ridden Keys): "She looks
around, and the water-skier isn't there anymore, then SNAP!
The whole boat goes . . ."

I especially like Joan, the svelte fortyish hostess, who turns
out to be a militant feminist, pulling me aside one day to
explain that "men run everything—we don't have a chance
unless we stick together." Accordingly, she backs me up when I
get overpowered on the floor, and in return I give her a chunk
of my tips or stand guard while she sneaks off for an unautho-
rized cigarette break. We all admire her for standing up to Billy
and telling him, after some of his usual nastiness about the
female server class, to "shut the fuck up." I even warm up to
Billy when, on a slow night and to make up for a particularly
unwarranted attack on my abilities, or so I imagine, he tells me
about his glory days as a young man at "coronary school" in
Brooklyn, where he dated a knockout Puerto Rican chick—or
do you say "culinary"?

I finish up every night at 10:00 or 10:30, depending on how
much side work I've been able to get done during the shift, and
cruise home to the tapes I snatched at random when I left my
real home—Marianne Faithfull, Tracy Chapman, Enigma,
King Sunny Adé, Violent Femmes—just drained enough for
the music to set my cranium resonating, but hardly dead. Midnight snack is Wheat Thins and Monterey Jack, accompanied
by cheap white wine on ice and whatever AMC has to offer. To
bed by 1:30 or 2:00, up at 9:00 or 10:00, read for an hour while
my uniform whirls around in the landlord's washing machine,
and then it's another eight hours spent following Mao's central
instruction, as laid out in the Little Red Book, which was:
Serve the people.

. . .

I COULD DRIFT ALONG LIKE THIS, IN SOME DREAMY PROLETARIAN idyll, except for two things. One is management. If I have kept this subject to the margins so far it is because I still flinch to think that I spent all those weeks under the surveillance of men (and later women) whose job it was to monitor my behavior for signs of sloth, theft, drug abuse, or worse. Not that managers and especially "assistant managers" in low-wage settings like this are exactly the class enemy. Mostly, in the restaurant business, they are former cooks still capable of pinch-hitting in the kitchen, just as in hotels they are likely to be former clerks, and paid a salary of only about $400 a week. But everyone knows they have crossed over to the other side, which is, crudely put, corporate as opposed to human. Cooks want to prepare tasty meals, servers want to serve them graciously, but managers are there for only one reason—to make sure that money is made for some theoretical entity, the corporation, which exists far away in Chicago or New York, if a corporation can be said to have a physical existence at all. Reflecting on her career, Gail tells me ruefully that she swore, years ago, never to work for a corporation again. "They don't cut you no slack. You give and you give and they take."

Managers can sit—for hours at a time if they want—but it's their job to see that no one else ever does, even when there's nothing to do, and this is why, for servers, slow times can be as exhausting as rushes. You start dragging out each little chore because if the manager on duty catches you in an idle moment he will give you something far nastier to do. So I wipe, I clean, I consolidate catsup bottles and recheck the cheesecake supply, even tour the tables to make sure the customer evaluation forms are all standing perkily in their places—wondering all the time how many calories I burn in these strictly theatrical exercises. In desperation, I even take the desserts out of their glass display case and freshen them up with whipped cream and bright new maraschino cherries; anything to look busy. When, on a particularly dead afternoon, Stu finds me glancing at a *USA Today* a customer has left behind, he assigns me to vacuum the entire floor with the broken vacuum cleaner, which has a handle only two feet long, and the only way to do that without incurring orthopedic damage is to proceed from spot to spot on your knees.

On my first Friday at Hearthside there is a "mandatory meeting for all restaurant employees," which I attend, eager for insight into our overall marketing strategy and the niche (your basic Ohio cuisine with a tropical twist?) we aim to inhabit. But there is no "we" at this meeting. Phillip, our top manager except for an occasional "consultant" sent out by corporate headquarters, opens it with a sneer: "The break room— it's disgusting. Butts in the ashtrays, newspapers lying around, crumbs." This windowless little room, which also houses the time clock for the entire hotel, is where we stash our bags and civilian clothes and take our half-hour meal breaks. But a break room is not a right, he tells us, it can be taken away. We should also know that the lockers in the break room and whatever is in them can be searched at any time. Then comes gossip; there has been gossip; gossip (which seems to mean employees talking among themselves) must stop. Off-duty employees are henceforth barred from eating at the restaurant, because "other servers gather around them and gossip." When Phillip has exhausted his agenda of rebukes, Joan complains about the condition of the ladies' room and I throw in my two bits about the vacuum cleaner. But I don't see any backup coming from my fellow servers, each of whom has slipped into her own personal funk; Gail, my role model, stares sorrowfully at a point six inches from her nose. The meeting ends when Andy, one of the cooks, gets up, muttering about breaking up his day off for this almighty bullshit.

Just four days later we are suddenly summoned into the kitchen at 3:30 P.M., even though there are live tables on the floor. We all—about ten of us—stand around Phillip, who announces grimly that there has been a report of some "drug activity" on the night shift and that, as a result, we are now to be a "drug-free" workplace, meaning that all new hires will be tested and possibly also current employees on a random basis. I am glad that this part of the kitchen is so dark because I find myself blushing as hard as if I had been caught toking up in the ladies' room myself: I haven't been treated this way—lined up in the corridor, threatened with locker searches, peppered with carelessly aimed accusations—since at least junior high school. Back on the floor, Joan cracks, "Next they'll be telling us we can't have *sex* on the job." When I ask Stu what happened to inspire the crackdown, he just mutters about "management decisions" and takes the opportunity to upbraid Gail and me for being too generous with the rolls. From now on there's to be only one per customer and it goes out with the dinner, not with the salad. He's also been riding the cooks, prompting Andy to come out of the kitchen and observe—with the serenity of a man whose customary implement is a butcher knife—that "Stu has a death wish today."

Later in the evening, the gossip crystallizes around the theory that Stu is himself the drug culprit, that he uses the restaurant phone to order up marijuana and sends one of the late servers out to fetch it for him. The server was caught and she may have ratted out Stu, at least enough to cast some suspicion on him, thus accounting for his pissy behavior. Who knows? Personally, I'm ready to believe anything bad about Stu, who serves no evident function and presumes too much on our common ethnicity, sidling up to me one night to engage in a little nativism directed at the Haitian immigrants: "I feel like I'm the foreigner here. They're taking over the country." Still later that evening, the drug in question escalates to crack. Lionel, the busboy, entertains us for the rest of the shift by standing just behind Stu's back and sucking deliriously on an imaginary joint or maybe a pipe.

The other problem, in addition to the less-than-nurturing management style, is that this job shows no sign of being financially viable. You might imagine, from a comfortable distance, that people who live, year in and year out, on $6 to $10 an hour have discovered some survival stratagems unknown to the middle class. But no. It's not hard to get my coworkers talking about their living situations, because housing, in almost every case, is the principal source of disruption in their lives, the first thing they fill you in on when they arrive for their shifts. After a week, I have compiled the following survey:

Gail is sharing a room in a well-known downtown flophouse for $250 a week. Her roommate, a male friend, has begun hitting on her, driving her nuts, but the rent would be impossible alone.

Claude, the Haitian cook, is desperate to get out of the two-room apartment he shares with his girlfriend and two other, unrelated people. As far as I can determine, the other Haitian men live in similarly crowded situations.

Annette, a twenty-year-old server who is six months pregnant and abandoned by her boyfriend, lives with her mother, a postal clerk.

Marianne, who is a breakfast server, and her boyfriend are paying $170 a week for a one-person trailer.

Billy, who at $10 an hour is the wealthiest of us, lives in the trailer he owns, paying only the $400-a-month lot fee.

The other white cook, Andy, lives on his dry-docked boat, which, as far as I can tell from his loving descriptions, can't be more than twenty feet long. He offers to take me out on it once it's repaired, but the offer comes with inquiries as to my marital status, so I do not follow up on it.

Tina, another server, and her husband are paying $60 a night for a room in the Days Inn. This is because they have no car and the Days Inn is in walking distance of the Hearthside. When Marianne is tossed out of her trailer for subletting (which is against trailer park rules), she leaves her boyfriend and moves in with Tina and her husband.

Joan, who had fooled me with her numerous and tasteful outfits (hostesses wear their own clothes), lives in a van parked behind a shopping center at night and showers in Tina's motel room. The clothes are from thrift shops.[3]

It strikes me, in my middle-class solipsism, that there is gross improvidence in some of these arrangements. When Gail and I are wrapping silverware in napkins—the only task for

---

[3] I could find no statistics on the number of employed people living in cars or vans, but according to a 1997 report of the National Coalition for the Homeless, "Myths and Facts about Homelessness," nearly one-fifth of all homeless people (in twenty-nine cities across the nation) are employed in full- or part-time jobs.

which we are permitted to sit—she tells me she is thinking of escaping from her roommate by moving into the Days Inn herself. I am astounded: how she can even think of paying $40 to $60 a day? But if I was afraid of sounding like a social worker, I have come out just sounding like a fool. She squints at me in disbelief: "And where am I supposed to get a month's rent and a month's deposit for an apartment?" I'd been feeling pretty smug about my $500 efficiency, but of course it was made possible only by the $1,300 I had allotted myself for start-up costs when I began my low-wage life: $1,000 for the first month's rent and deposit, $100 for initial groceries and cash in my pocket, $200 stuffed away for emergencies. In poverty, as in certain propositions in physics, starting conditions are everything.

There are no secret economies that nourish the poor; on the contrary, there are a host of special costs. If you can't put up the two months' rent you need to secure an apartment, you end up paying through the nose for a room by the week. If you have only a room, with a hot plate at best, you can't save by cooking up huge lentil stews that can be frozen for the week ahead. You eat fast food or the hot dogs and Styrofoam cups of soup that can be microwaved in a convenience store. If you have no money for health insurance—and the Hearthside's niggardly plan kicks in only after three months—you go without routine care or prescription drugs and end up paying the price. Gail, for example, was doing fine, healthwise anyway, until she ran out of money for estrogen pills. She is supposed to be on the company health plan by now, but they claim to have lost her application form and to be beginning the paperwork all over again. So she spends $9 a pop for pills to control the migraines she wouldn't have, she insists, if her estrogen supplements were covered. Similarly, Marianne's boyfriend lost his job as a roofer because he missed so much time after getting a cut on his foot for which he couldn't afford the prescribed antibiotic.

My own situation, when I sit down to assess it after two weeks of work, would not be much better if this were my actual life. The seductive thing about waitressing is that you don't have to wait for payday to feel a few bills in your pocket, and my tips usually cover meals and gas, plus something left over to stuff into the kitchen drawer I use as a bank. But as the tourist business slows in the summer heat, I sometimes leave work with only $20 in tips (the gross is higher, but servers share about 15 percent of their tips with the busboys and bartenders). With wages included, this amounts to about the minimum wage of $5.15 an hour. The sum in the drawer is piling up but at the present rate of accumulation will be more than $100 short of my rent when the end of the month comes around. Nor can I see any expenses to cut. True, I haven't gone the lentil stew route yet, but that's because I don't have a large cooking pot, potholders, or a ladle to stir with (which would cost a total of about $30 at Kmart, somewhat less at a thrift store), not to mention onions, carrots, and the indispensable bay leaf. I do make my lunch almost every day—usually some slow-burning, high-protein combo like frozen chicken patties with melted cheese on top and canned pinto beans on the side. Dinner is at the Hearthside, which offers its employees a choice of BLT, fish sandwich, or hamburger for only $2. The burger lasts longest, especially if it's heaped with gut-puckering jalapeños, but by midnight my stomach is growling again.

So unless I want to start using my car as a residence, I have to find a second or an alternative job. I call all the hotels I'd filled out housekeeping applications at weeks ago—the Hyatt, Holiday Inn, Econo Lodge, HoJo's, Best Western, plus a half dozen locally run guest houses. Nothing. Then I start making the rounds again, wasting whole mornings waiting for some assistant manager to show up, even dipping into places so creepy that the front-desk clerk greets you from behind bullet-proof glass and sells pints of liquor over the counter. But either someone has exposed my real-life housekeeping habits—which are, shall we say, mellow—or I am at the wrong end of some infallible ethnic equation: most, but by no means all, of the working housekeepers I see on my job searches are African Americans, Spanish-speaking, or refugees from the Central European post-Communist world, while servers are almost invariably white and monolingually English-speaking. When I finally get a positive response, I have been identified once again as server material. Jerry's—again, not the real name—which is part of a well-known national chain and physically attached here to another budget hotel, is ready to use me at once. The prospect is both exciting and terrifying because, with about the same number of tables and counter seats, Jerry's attracts three or four times the volume of customers as the gloomy old Hearthside.

PICTURE A FAT PERSON'S HELL, AND I DON'T MEAN A PLACE WITH NO food. Instead there is everything you might eat if eating had no bodily consequences—the cheese fries, the chicken-fried steaks, the fudge-laden desserts—only here every bite must be paid for, one way or another, in human discomfort. The kitchen is a cavern, a stomach leading to the lower intestine that is the garbage and dishwashing area, from which issue bizarre smells combining the edible and the offal: creamy carrion, pizza barf, and that unique and enigmatic Jerry's scent, citrus fart. The floor is slick with spills, forcing us to walk through the kitchen with tiny steps, like Susan McDougal in leg irons. Sinks everywhere are clogged with scraps of lettuce, decomposing lemon wedges, water-logged toast crusts. Put your hand down on any counter and you risk being stuck to it by the film of ancient syrup spills, and this is unfortunate because hands are utensils here, used for scooping up lettuce onto the salad plates, lifting out pie slices, and even moving hash browns from one plate to another. The regulation poster in the single unisex rest room admonishes us to wash our hands thoroughly, and even offers instructions for doing so, but there is always some vital substance missing—soap, paper towels, toilet paper—and I never found all three at once. You learn to stuff your pockets with napkins before going in there, and too bad about the customers, who must eat, although they don't realize it, almost literally out of our hands.

The break room summarizes the whole situation: there is none, because there are no breaks at Jerry's. For six to eight hours in a row, you never sit except to pee. Actually, there are three folding chairs at a table immediately adjacent to the bathroom, but hardly anyone ever sits in this, the very rectum of the gastroarchitectural system. Rather, the function of the peri-toilet area is to house the ashtrays in which servers and dishwashers leave their cigarettes burning at all times, like votive candles, so they don't have to waste time lighting up again when they dash back here for a puff. Almost everyone smokes as if their pulmonary well-being depended on it—the multinational mélange of cooks; the dishwashers, who are all Czechs here; the servers, who are American natives—creating an atmosphere in which oxygen is only an occasional pollutant. My first morning at Jerry's, when the hypoglycemic shakes set in,

I complain to one of my fellow servers that I don't understand how she can go so long without food. "Well, I don't understand how *you* can go so long without a cigarette," she responds in a tone of reproach. Because work is what you do for others; smoking is what you do for yourself. I don't know why the antismoking crusaders have never grasped the element of defiant self-nurturance that makes the habit so endearing to its victims—as if, in the American workplace, the only thing people have to call their own is the tumors they are nourishing and the spare moments they devote to feeding them.

Now, the Industrial Revolution is not an easy transition, especially, in my experience, when you have to zip through it in just a couple of days. I have gone from craft work straight into the factory, from the air-conditioned morgue of the Hearthside directly into the flames. Customers arrive in human waves, sometimes disgorged fifty at a time from their tour buses, peckish and whiny. Instead of two "girls" on the floor at once, there can be as many as six of us running around in our brilliant pink-and-orange Hawaiian shirts. Conversations, either with customers or with fellow employees, seldom last more than twenty seconds at a time. On my first day, in fact, I am hurt by my sister servers' coldness. My mentor for the day is a supremely competent, emotionally uninflected twenty-three-year-old, and the others, who gossip a little among themselves about the real reason someone is out sick today and the size of the bail bond someone else has had to pay, ignore me completely. On my second day, I find out why. "Well, it's good to see *you* again," one of them says in greeting. "Hardly anyone comes back after the first day." I feel powerfully vindicated—a survivor—but it would take a long time, probably months, before I could hope to be accepted into this sorority.

I start out with the beautiful, heroic idea of handling the two jobs at once, and for two days I almost do it: working the breakfast/lunch shift at Jerry's from 8:00 till 2:00, arriving at the Hearthside a few minutes late, at 2:10, and attempting to hold out until 10:00. In the few minutes I have between jobs, I pick up a spicy chicken sandwich at the Wendy's drive-through window, gobble it down in the car, and change from khaki slacks to black, from Hawaiian to rust-colored polo. There is a problem, though. When, during the 3:00–4:00 o'clock dead time, I finally sit down to wrap silver, my flesh seems to bond to the seat. I try to refuel with a purloined cup of clam chowder, as I've seen Gail and Joan do dozens of time, but Stu catches me and hisses "No *eating*!" although there's not a customer around to be offended by the sight of food making contact with a server's lips. So I tell Gail I'm going to quit, and she hugs me and says she might just follow me to Jerry's herself.

But the chances of this are minuscule. She has left the flop-house and her annoying roommate and is back to living in her truck. But, guess what, she reports to me excitedly later that evening, Phillip has given her permission to park overnight in the hotel parking lot, as long as she keeps out of sight, and the parking lot should be totally safe since it's patrolled by a hotel security guard! With the Hearthside offering benefits like that, how could anyone think of leaving? This must be Phillip's theory, anyway. He accepts my resignation with a shrug, his main concern being that I return my two polo shirts and aprons.

Gail would have triumphed at Jerry's, I'm sure, but for me it's a crash course in exhaustion management. Years ago, the kindly fry cook who trained me to waitress at a Los Angeles truck stop used to say: Never make an unnecessary trip; if you don't have to walk fast, walk slow; if you don't have to walk, stand. But at Jerry's the effort of distinguishing necessary from unnecessary and urgent from whenever would itself be too much of an energy drain. The only thing to do is to treat each shift as a one-time-only emergency: you've got fifty starving people out there, lying scattered on the battlefield, so get out there and feed them! Forget that you will have to do this again tomorrow, forget that you will have to be alert enough to dodge the drunks on the drive home tonight—just burn, burn, burn! Ideally, at some point you enter what servers call a "rhythm" and psychologists term a "flow state," where signals pass from the sense organs directly to the muscles, bypassing the cerebral cortex, and a Zen-like emptiness sets in. I'm on a 2:00–10:00 P.M. shift now, and a male server from the morning shift tells me about the time he "pulled a triple"—three shifts in a row, all the way around the clock—and then got off and had a drink and met this girl, and maybe he shouldn't tell me this, but they had sex right then and there and it was like *beautiful*.

But there's another capacity of the neuromuscular system, which is pain. I start tossing back drugstore-brand ibuprofens as if they were vitamin C, four before each shift, because an old mouse-related repetitive-stress injury in my upper back has come back to full-spasm strength, thanks to the tray carrying. In my ordinary life, this level of disability might justify a day of ice packs and stretching. Here I comfort myself with the Aleve commercial where the cute blue-collar guy asks: If you quit after working four hours, what would your boss say? And the not-so-cute blue-collar guy, who's lugging a metal beam on his back, answers: He'd fire me, that's what. But fortunately, the commercial tells us, we workers can exert the same kind of authority over our painkillers that our bosses exert over us. If

Tylenol doesn't want to work for more than four hours, you just fire its ass and switch to Aleve.

True, I take occasional breaks from this life, going home now and then to catch up on e-mail and for conjugal visits (though I am careful to "pay" for everything I eat here, at $5 for a dinner, which I put in a jar), seeing *The Truman Show* with friends and letting them buy my ticket. And I still have those what-am-I-doing-here moments at work, when I get so homesick for the printed word that I obsessively reread the six-page menu. But as the days go by, my old life is beginning to look exceedingly strange. The e-mails and phone messages addressed to my former self come from a distant race of people with exotic concerns and far too much time on their hands. The neighborly market I used to cruise for produce now looks forbiddingly like a Manhattan yuppie emporium. And when I sit down one morning in my real home to pay bills from my past life, I am dazzled by the two- and three-figure sums owed to outfits like Club Body Tech and Amazon.com.

Management at Jerry's is generally calmer and more "professional" than at the Hearthside, with two exceptions. One is Joy, a plump, blowsy woman in her early thirties who once kindly devoted several minutes of her time to instructing me in the correct one-handed method of tray carrying but whose moods change disconcertingly from shift to shift and even within one. The other is B.J., aka B.J. the Bitch, whose contribution is to stand by the kitchen counter and yell, "Nita, your order's up, move it!" or "Barbara, didn't you see you've got another table out there? Come *on,* girl!" Among other things, she is hated for having replaced the whipped cream squirt cans with big plastic whipped-cream-filled baggies that have to be squeezed with both hands—because, reportedly, she saw or thought she saw employees trying to inhale the propellant gas from the squirt cans, in the hope that it might be nitrous oxide. On my third night, she pulls me aside abruptly and brings her face so close that it looks like she's planning to butt me with her forehead. But instead of saying "You're fired," she says, "You're doing fine." The only trouble is I'm spending time chatting with customers: "That's how they're getting you." Furthermore I am letting them "run me," which means harassment by sequential demands: you bring the catsup and they decide they want extra Thousand Island; you bring that and they announce they now need a side of fries, and so on into distraction. Finally she tells me not to take her wrong. She tries to say things in a nice way, but "you get into a mode, you know, because everything has to move so fast."[4]

I mumble thanks for the advice, feeling like I've just been stripped naked by the crazed enforcer of some ancient sumptuary law: No chatting for *you,* girl. No fancy service ethic allowed for the serfs. Chatting with customers is for the good-looking young college-educated servers in the downtown carpaccio and ceviche joints, the kids who can make $70–$100 a night. What had I been thinking? My job is to move orders from tables to kitchen and then trays from kitchen to tables. Customers are in fact the major obstacle to the smooth transformation of information into food and food into money—they are, in short, the enemy. And the painful thing is that I'm

[4] In *Workers in a Lean World: Unions in the International Economy* (Verso, 1997), Kim Moody cites studies finding an increase in stress-related workplace injuries and illness between the mid-1980s and the early 1990s. He argues that rising stress levels reflect a new system of "management by stress" in which workers in a variety of industries are being squeezed to extract maximum productivity, to the detriment of their health.

beginning to see it this way myself. There are the traditional asshole types—frat boys who down multiple Buds and then make a fuss because the steaks are so emaciated and the fries so sparse—as well as the variously impaired—due to age, diabetes, or literacy issues—who require patient nutritional counseling. The worst, for some reason, are the Visible Christians—like the ten-person table, all jolly and sanctified after Sunday night service, who run me mercilessly and then leave me $1 on a $92 bill. Or the guy with the crucifixion T-shirt (SOMEONE TO LOOK UP TO) who complains that his baked potato is too hard and his iced tea too icy (I cheerfully fix both) and leaves no tip at all. As a general rule, people wearing crosses or WWJD? ("What Would Jesus Do?") buttons look at us disapprovingly no matter what we do, as if they were confusing waitressing with Mary Magdalene's original profession.

I make friends, over time, with the other "girls" who work my shift: Nita, the tattooed twenty-something who taunts us by going around saying brightly, "Have we started making money yet?" Ellen, whose teenage son cooks on the graveyard shift and who once managed a restaurant in Massachusetts but won't try out for management here because she prefers being a "common worker" and not "ordering people around." Easygoing fiftyish Lucy, with the raucous laugh, who limps toward the end of the shift because of something that has gone wrong with her leg, the exact nature of which cannot be determined without health insurance. We talk about the usual girl things— men, children, and the sinister allure of Jerry's chocolate peanut-butter cream pie—though no one, I notice, ever brings up anything potentially expensive, like shopping or movies. As at the Hearthside, the only recreation ever referred to is partying, which requires little more than some beer, a joint, and a few close friends. Still, no one is homeless, or cops to it anyway, thanks usually to a working husband or boyfriend. All in all, we form a reliable mutual-support group: if one of us is feeling sick or overwhelmed, another one will "bev" a table or even carry trays for her. If one of us is off sneaking a cigarette or a pee, the others will do their best to conceal her absence from the enforcers of corporate rationality.[5]

But my saving human connection—my oxytocin receptor, as it were—is George, the nineteen-year-old Czech dishwasher who has been in this country exactly one week. We get talking when he asks me, tortuously, how much cigarettes cost at Jerry's. I do my best to explain that they cost over a dollar more here than at a regular store and suggest that he just take one from the half-filled packs that are always lying around on the break table. But that would be unthinkable. Except for the one tiny earring signaling his allegiance to some vaguely alternative point of view, George is a perfect straight arrow—crew-cut, hardworking, and hungry for eye contact. "Czech Republic," I ask, "or Slovakia?" and he seems delighted that I know the difference. "Vaclav Havel," I try, "Velvet Revolution, Frank

---

[5] Until April 1998, there was no federally mandated right to bathroom breaks. According to Marc Linder and Ingrid Nygaard, authors of *Void Where Prohibited: Rest Breaks and the Right to Urinate on Company Time* (Cornell University Press, 1997), "The right to rest and void at work is not high on the list of social or political causes supported by professional or executive employees, who enjoy personal workplace liberties that millions of factory workers can only dream about. . . . While we were dismayed to discover that workers lacked an acknowledged right to void at work, [the workers] were amazed by outsiders' naïve belief that their employers would permit them to perform this basic bodily function when necessary. . . . A factory worker, not allowed a break for six-hour stretches, voided into pads worn inside her uniform; and a kindergarten teacher in a school without aides had to take all twenty children with her to the bathroom and line them up outside the stall door while she voided."

Zappa?" "Yes, yes, 1989," he says, and I realize that for him this is already history.

My project is to teach George English. "How are you today, George?" I say at the start of each shift. "I am good, and how are you today, Barbara?" I learn that he is not paid by Jerry's but by the "agent" who shipped him over—$5 an hour, with the agent getting the dollar or so difference between that and what Jerry's pays dishwashers. I learn also that he shares an apartment with a crowd of other Czech "dishers," as he calls them, and that he cannot sleep until one of them goes off for his shift, leaving a vacant bed. We are having one of our ESL sessions late one afternoon when B.J. catches us at it and orders "Joseph" to take up the rubber mats on the floor near the dishwashing sinks and mop underneath. "I thought your name was George," I say loud enough for B.J. to hear as she strides off back to the counter. Is she embarrassed? Maybe a little, because she greets me back at the counter with "George, Joseph—there are so many of them!" I say nothing, neither nodding nor smiling, and for this I am punished later, when I think I am ready to go and she announces that I need to roll fifty more sets of silverware, and isn't it time I mixed up a fresh four-gallon batch of blue-cheese dressing? May you grow old in this place, B.J., is the curse I beam out at her when I am finally permitted to leave. May the syrup spills glue your feet to the floor.

I make the decision to move closer to Key West. First, because of the drive. Second and third, also because of the drive: gas is eating up $4–$5 a day, and although Jerry's is as high-volume as you can get, the tips average only 10 percent, and not just for a newbie like me. Between the base pay of $2.15 an hour and the obligation to share tips with the busboys and dishwashers, we're averaging only about $7.50 an hour. Then there is the $30 I had to spend on the regulation tan slacks worn by Jerry's servers—a setback it could take weeks to absorb. (I had combed the town's two downscale department stores hoping for something cheaper but decided in the end that these marked-down Dockers, originally $49, were more likely to survive a daily washing.) Of my fellow servers, everyone who lacks a working husband or boyfriend seems to have a second job: Nita does something at a computer eight hours a day; another welds. Without the forty-five-minute commute, I can picture myself working two jobs and still having the time to shower between them.

So I take the $500 deposit I have coming from my landlord, the $400 I have earned toward the next month's rent, plus the $200 reserved for emergencies, and use the $1,100 to pay the rent and deposit on trailer number 46 in the Overseas Trailer Park, a mile from the cluster of budget hotels that constitute Key West's version of an industrial park. Number 46 is about eight feet in width and shaped like a barbell inside, with a narrow region—because of the sink and the stove—separating the bedroom from what might optimistically be called the "living" area, with its two-person table and half-sized couch. The bathroom is so small my knees rub against the shower stall when I sit on the toilet, and you can't just leap out of the bed, you have to climb down to the foot of it in order to find a patch of floor space to stand on. Outside, I am within a few yards of a liquor store, a bar that advertises "free beer tomorrow," a convenience store, and a Burger King—but no supermarket or, alas, Laundromat. By reputation, the Overseas park is a nest of crime and crack, and I am hoping at least for some vibrant multicultural street life. But desolation rules night and day, except for a thin stream of pedestrians heading for their jobs at the Sheraton or the 7-Eleven. There are not exactly people here but what amounts to canned labor, being preserved between shifts from the heat.

In line with my reduced living conditions, a new form of ugliness arises at Jerry's. First we are confronted—via an announcement on the computers through which we input orders—with the new rule that the hotel bar, the Driftwood, is henceforth off-limits to restaurant employees. The culprit, I learn through the grapevine, is the ultraefficient twenty-three-year-old who trained me—another trailer home dweller and a mother of three. Something had set her off one morning, so she slipped out for a nip and returned to the floor impaired. The restriction mostly hurts Ellen, whose habit it is to free her hair from its rubber band and drop by the Driftwood for a couple of Zins before heading home at the end of her shift, but all of us feel the chill. Then the next day, when I go for straws, I find the dry-storage room locked. It's never been locked before; we go in and out of it all day—for napkins, jelly containers, Styrofoam cups for takeout. Vic, the portly assistant manager who opens it for me, explains that he caught one of the dishwashers attempting to steal something and, unfortunately, the miscreant will be with us until a replacement can be found—hence the locked door. I neglect to ask what he had been trying to steal but Vic tells me who he is—the kid with the buzz cut and the earring, you know, he's back there right now.

I wish I could say I rushed back and confronted George to get his side of the story. I wish I could say I stood up to Vic and insisted that George be given a translator and allowed to defend himself or announced that I'd find a lawyer who'd handle the case pro bono. At the very least I should have testified as to the kid's honesty. The mystery to me is that there's not much worth stealing in the dry-storage room, at least not in any fenceable quantity: "Is Gyorgi here, and am having 200—maybe 250—catsup packets. What do you say?" My guess is that he had taken—if he had taken anything at all—some Saltines or a can of cherry pie mix and that the motive for taking it was hunger.

So why didn't I intervene? Certainly not because I was held back by the kind of moral paralysis that can mask as journalistic objectivity. On the contrary, something new—something loathsome and servile—had infected me, along with the kitchen odors that I could still sniff on my bra when I finally undressed at night. In real life I am moderately brave, but plenty of brave people shed their courage in POW camps, and maybe something similar goes on in the infinitely more congenial milieu of the low-wage American workplace. Maybe, in a month or two more at Jerry's, I might have regained my crusading spirit. Then again, in a month or two I might have turned into a different person altogether—say, the kind of person who would have turned George in.

But this is not something I was slated to find out. When my monthlong plunge into poverty was almost over, I finally landed my dream job—housekeeping. I did this by walking into the personnel office of the only place I figured I might have some credibility, the hotel attached to Jerry's, and confiding urgently that I had to have a second job if I was to pay my rent and, no, it couldn't be front-desk clerk. "All *right*," the personnel lady fairly spits, "so it's *housekeeping,*" and marches me back to meet Millie, the housekeeping manager, a tiny, frenetic Hispanic woman who greets me as "babe" and hands me a pamphlet emphasizing the need for a positive attitude. The pay is $6.10 an hour and the hours are nine in the morning till "whenever," which I am hoping can be defined as a little before two. I don't have to ask about health insurance once I meet Carlotta, the middle-aged African American woman who will be training me. Carlie, as she tells me to call her, is missing all of her top front teeth.

ON THAT FIRST DAY OF HOUSEKEEPING AND LAST DAY—ALTHOUGH I don't yet know it's the last—of my life as a low-wage worker in Key West, Carlie is in a foul mood. We have been given nineteen rooms to clean, most of them "checkouts," as opposed to "stay-overs," and requiring the whole enchilada of bed stripping, vacuuming, and bathroom scrubbing. When one of the rooms that had been listed as a stay-over turns out to be a checkout, she calls Millie to complain, but of course to no avail. "So make up the motherfucker," she orders me, and I do the beds while she sloshes around the bathroom. For four hours without a break I strip and remake beds, taking about four and a half minutes per queen-sized bed, which I could get down to three if there were any reason to. We try to avoid vacuuming by picking up the larger specks by hand, but often there is nothing to do but drag the monstrous vacuum cleaner—it weighs about thirty pounds—off our cart and try to wrestle it around the floor. Sometimes Carlie hands me the squirt bottle of "Bam" (an acronym for something that begins, ominously, with "butyric"—the rest of it has been worn off the label) and lets me do the bathrooms. No service ethic challenges me here to new heights of performance. I just concentrate on removing the pubic hairs from the bathtubs, or at least the dark ones that I can see.

I had looked forward to the breaking-and-entering aspect of cleaning the stay-overs, the chance to examine the secret physical existence of strangers. But the contents of the rooms are always banal and surprisingly neat—zipped-up shaving kits, shoes lined up against the wall (there are no closets), flyers for snorkeling trips, maybe an empty wine bottle or two. It is the TV that keeps us going, from Jerry to Sally to *Hawaii Five-0* and then on to the soaps. If there's something especially arresting, like "Won't Take No for an Answer" on Jerry, we sit down on the edge of a bed and giggle for a moment, as if this were a pajama party instead of a terminally dead-end job. The soaps are the best, and Carlie turns the volume up full blast so she won't miss anything from the bathroom or while the vacuum is on. In Room 503, Marcia confronts Jeff about Lauren. In 505, Lauren taunts poor cheated-on Marcia. In 511, Helen offers Amanda $10,000 to stop seeing Eric, prompting Carlie to emerge from the bathroom to study Amanda's troubled face. "You take it, girl," she advises. "I would for sure."

The tourists' rooms that we clean and, beyond them, the far more expensively appointed interiors in the soaps begin after a while to merge. We have entered a better world—a world of comfort where every day is a day off, waiting to be filled with sexual intrigue. We are only gate-crashers in this fantasy, however, forced to pay for our presence with backaches and perpetual thirst. The mirrors, and there are far too many of them in hotel rooms, contain the kind of person you would normally find pushing a shopping cart down a city street—bedraggled, dressed in a damp hotel polo shirt two sizes too large, and with sweat dribbling down her chin like drool. I am enormously relieved when Carlie announces a half-hour meal break, but my appetite fades when I see that the bag of hot dog rolls she has been carrying around on our cart is not trash salvaged from a checkout but what she has brought for her lunch.

Between the TV and the fact that I'm in no position, as a first dayer, to launch new topics of conversation, I don't learn much about Carlie except that she hurts, and in more than one way. She moves slowly about her work, muttering something about joint pain, and this is probably going to doom her, since the young immigrant housekeepers—Polish and Salvadoran—like to polish off their rooms by two in the afternoon, while she drags the work out till six. It doesn't make any sense to hurry, she observes, when you're being paid by the hour. Already, management has brought in a woman to do what sounds like time-motion studies and there's talk about switching to paying by the room.[6] She broods, too, about all the little evidences of disrespect that come her way, and not only from management. "They don't care about us," she tells me of the hotel guests; in fact, they don't notice us at all unless something gets stolen from a room—"then they're all over you." We're eating our lunch side by side in the break room when a white guy in a maintenance uniform walks by and Carlie calls out, "Hey you," in a friendly way, "what's your name?"

"Peter Pan," he says, his back already to us.

"That wasn't funny," Carlie says, turning to me. "That was no kind of answer. Why did he have to be funny like that?" I venture that he has an attitude, and she nods as if that were an acute diagnosis. "Yeah, he got a attitude all right."

---

[6] A few weeks after I left, I heard ads on the radio for housekeeping jobs at this hotel at the amazing rate of "up to $9 an hour." When I inquired, I found out that the hotel had indeed started paying by the room, and I suspect that Carlie, if she lasted, was still making the equivalent of $6 an hour or quite a bit less.

"Maybe he's a having a bad day," I elaborate, not because I feel any obligation to defend the white race but because her face is so twisted with hurt.

When I request permission to leave at about 3:30, another housekeeper warns me that no one has so far succeeded in combining housekeeping with serving at Jerry's: "Some kid did it once for five days, and you're no kid." With that helpful information in mind, I rush back to number 46, down four Advils (the name brand this time), shower, stooping to fit into the stall, and attempt to compose myself for the oncoming shift. So much for what Marx termed the "reproduction of labor power," meaning the things a worker has to do just so she'll be ready to labor again. The only unforeseen obstacle to the smooth transition from job to job is that my tan Jerry's slacks, which had looked reasonably clean by 40-watt bulb last night when I hand washed my Hawaiian shirt, prove by daylight to be mottled with catsup and ranch-dressing stains. I spend most of my hour-long break between jobs attempting to remove the edible portions of the slacks with a sponge and then drying them over the hood of my car in the sun.

I can do this two-job thing, is my theory, if I can drink enough caffeine and avoid getting distracted by George's ever more obvious suffering.[7] The first few days after the alleged theft, he seemed not to understand the trouble he was in, and

[7] In 1996 the number of persons holding two or more jobs averaged 7.8 million, or 6.2 percent of the workforce. It was about the same rate for men and for women (6.1 versus 6.2). About two-thirds of multiple jobholders work one job full-time and the other part-time. Only a heroic minority—4 percent of men and 2 percent of women—work two full-time jobs simultaneously (John F. Stinson Jr., "New Data on Multiple Jobholding Available from the CPS," *Monthly Labor Review,* March 1997).

our chirpy little conversations had continued. But the last
couple of shifts he's been listless and unshaven, and tonight he
looks like the ghost we all know him to be, with dark half-
moons hanging from his eyes. At one point, when I am briefly
immobilized by the task of filling little paper cups with sour
cream for baked potatoes, he comes over and looks as if he'd
like to explore the limits of our shared vocabulary, but I am
called to the floor for a table. I resolve to give him all my tips
that night, and to hell with the experiment in low-wage money
management. At eight, Ellen and I grab a snack together standing at the mephitic end of the kitchen counter, but I can only
manage two or three mozzarella sticks, and lunch had been a
mere handful of McNuggets. I am not tired at all, I assure
myself, though it may be that there is simply no more "I" left to
do the tiredness monitoring. What I would see if I were more
alert to the situation is that the forces of destruction are already
massing against me. There is only one cook on duty, a young
man named Jesus ("Hay-Sue," that is), and he is new to the job.
And there is Joy, who shows up to take over in the middle of
the shift dressed in high heels and a long, clingy white dress
and fuming as if she'd just been stood up in some cocktail bar.

Then it comes, the perfect storm. Four of my tables fill up at
once. Four tables is nothing for me now, but only so long as
they are obligingly staggered. As I bev table 27, tables 25, 28,
and 24 are watching enviously. As I bev 25, 24 glowers because
their bevs haven't even been ordered. Twenty-eight is four
yuppyish types, meaning everything on the side and agonizing
instructions as to the chicken Caesars. Twenty-five is a middle-
aged black couple who complain, with some justice, that the
iced tea isn't fresh and the tabletop is sticky. But table 24 is the

meteorological event of the century: ten British tourists who seem to have made the decision to absorb the American experience entirely by mouth. Here everyone has at least two drinks—iced tea *and* milk shake, Michelob *and* water (with lemon slice in the water, please)—and a huge, promiscuous orgy of breakfast specials, mozz sticks, chicken strips, quesadillas, burgers with cheese and without, sides of hash browns with cheddar, with onions, with gravy, seasoned fries, plain fries, banana splits. Poor Jesus! Poor me! Because when I arrive with their first tray of food—after three prior trips just to refill bevs—Princess Di refuses to eat her chicken strips with her pancake and sausage special since, as she now reveals, the strips were meant to be an appetizer. Maybe the others would have accepted their meals, but Di, who is deep into her third Michelob, insists that everything else go back while they work on their starters. Meanwhile, the yuppies are waving me down for more decaf and the black couple looks ready to summon the NAACP.

Much of what happens next is lost in the fog of war. Jesus starts going under. The little printer in front of him is spewing out orders faster than he can rip them off, much less produce the meals. A menacing restlessness rises from the tables, all of which are full. Even the invincible Ellen is ashen from stress. I take table 24 their reheated main courses, which they immediately reject as either too cold or fossilized by the microwave. When I return to the kitchen with their trays (three trays in three trips) Joy confronts me with arms akimbo: "What *is* this?" She means the food—the plates of rejected pancakes, hash browns in assorted flavors, toasts, burgers, sausages, eggs. "Uh, scrambled with cheddar," I try, "and that's—" *"No,"* she screams in my face, "is it a traditional, a super-scramble, an eye-opener?" I pretend to study my check for a clue, but entropy has been up to its tricks, not only on the plates but in my head, and I have to admit that the original order is beyond reconstruction. "You don't know an eye-opener from a traditional?" she demands in outrage. All I know, in fact, is that my legs have lost interest in the current venture and have announced their intention to fold. I am saved by a yuppie (mercifully not one of mine) who chooses this moment to charge into the kitchen to bellow that his food is twenty-five minutes late. Joy screams at him to get the hell out of her kitchen, *please,* and then turns on Jesus in a fury, hurling an empty tray across the room for emphasis.

I leave. I don't walk out, I just leave. I don't finish my side work or pick up my credit card tips, if any, at the cash register or, of course, ask Joy's permission to go. And the surprising thing is that you *can* walk out without permission, that the door opens, that the thick tropical night air parts to let me pass, that my car is still parked where I left it. There is no vindication in this exit, no fuck-you surge of relief, just an overwhelming dank sense of failure pressing down on me and the entire parking lot. I had gone into this venture in the spirit of science, to test a mathematical proposition, but somewhere along the line, in the tunnel vision imposed by long shifts and relentless concentration, it became a test of myself, and clearly I have failed. Not only had I flamed out as a housekeeper/ server, I had forgotten to give George my tips, and, for reasons perhaps best known to hardworking, generous people like Gail and Ellen, this hurts. I don't cry, but I am in a position to realize, for the first time in many years, that the tear ducts are still there and still capable of doing their job.

. . .

WHEN I MOVED OUT OF THE TRAILER PARK, I GAVE THE KEY TO number 46 to Gail and arranged for my deposit to be transferred to her. She told me that Joan was still living in her van and that Stu had been fired from the Hearthside. According to the most up-to-date rumors, the drug he ordered from the restaurant was crack and he was caught dipping into the cash register to pay for it. I never found out what happened to George.

two

Scrubbing in Maine

I chose Maine for its whiteness. A few months back, in the spring, I had been in the Portland area for a speaking engagement at a local college and was struck by what appeared to be an extreme case of demographic albinism. Not only were the professors and students white, which is of course not uncommon; so were the hotel housekeepers, the panhandlers, and the cab drivers, who, in addition to being white, also spoke English, or at least some *r*-less New England variant thereof. This might not make Maine an ideal setting in which to hunker down for the long haul, but it made it the perfect place for a blue-eyed, English-speaking Caucasian to infiltrate the low-wage workforce, no questions asked. As an additional attraction, I noted on my spring visit that the Portland-area business community was begging piteously for fresh employable bodies. Local TV news encouraged viewers to try out for a telemarketing firm offering a special "mothers' shift"; the classic rock station was promoting "job fairs" where you could stroll among the employers' tables, like a shopper at the mall, playing hard to get. Before deciding to return to Maine as an entry-level worker, I downloaded the help-wanted ads from the *Portland Press Herald*'s Web site, and my desktop wheezed from the strain. At least three of the thousand or so ads I scanned promised "fun, casual" workplace environments, and I pictured flannel-shirted teams bantering on their afternoon cider-and-doughnut breaks. Maybe, I reasoned, when you give white people a whole state to themselves, they treat one another real nice.

On the evening of Tuesday, August 24, still summer but with back-to-school sales shouting for attention from every shopping center, I arrive at the Trailways bus station in Portland and take a cab, since it's too late in the day to pick up my Rent-A-Wreck, to the Motel 6 that will be my base until I find the perquisites of normal citizenship—job and home. This is, admittedly, an odd venture for anyone not involved in a witness-protection program: to leave home and companionship and plop down nearly two thousand miles away in a place where I know almost no one and about which I am ignorant right down to the most elementary data on geography, weather, and good places to eat. Still, I reason, this sudden removal to an unknown state is not all that different from the kinds of dislocations that routinely segment the lives of the truly poor. You lose your job, your car, or your babysitter. Or maybe you lose your home because you've been living with a mother or a sister who throws you out when her boyfriend comes back or because she needs the bed or sofa you've been sleeping on for some other wayward family member. And there you are. And here I am—as clueless and alone as I have ever been in my grown-up life.

One of the steps A.A. asks of recovering alcoholics is to make "a searching and fearless moral inventory" of themselves, and now, alone in my motel room, I find myself fairly obsessed with my *stuff,* how much of it there is and how long it will last. I have my laptop and a suitcase containing T-shirts, jeans, and khakis, three long-sleeve shirts, one pair of shorts, vitamins, and an assortment of toiletries. I have a tote bag stuffed with books, which will, along with the hiking boots I have brought for weekends, turn out to be the most useless items in my inventory. I have $1,000, plus some small bills crumpled in pockets. And now, for an alarming $59 a night, I have a bed, a TV, a phone, and a nearly unobstructed view of Route 25. There are two kinds of low-rent motel rooms in America: the Hampton Inn type, which are clearly *calibrated,* rather than decorated, to produce an atmosphere of menacing sterility—and the other kind, in which history has been allowed to accumulate in the form of carpet stains, lingering deposits of cigarette smoke, and Cheeto crumbs deep under the bed. This Motel 6 is in the latter category, which makes it homier, you might say, or maybe only more haunted. Walking out from the main entrance, through the VIP Auto Parts parking lot, you reach the Texaco station with a Clipper Mart attached. Crossing the turnpike from the Texaco—a feat that, performed on foot, demands both speed and nerve—brings you to more substantial sources of sustenance, including a Pizza Hut and a Shop-n-Save. This is, of course, a considerable step up from the situation described in J. G. Ballard's harrowing novel *Concrete Island,* in which the hero crashes onto a median island and finds himself marooned by the traffic, forced to live off the contents of his car and what-ever food items he can scrounge from the debris left by motorists. I bring pizza and salad back to my room for dinner, telling myself that anything tastes better when acquired at some risk to life and limb, like venison fresh from the hunt.

How many people, other than fugitives and refugees, ever get to do something like this—blow off all past relationships and routines, say bye-bye to those mounds of unanswered mail and voice-mail messages, and start all over again, with not much more than a driver's license and a Social Security card to provide a thread of continuity to the past? This should be exhilarating, I tell myself, like a dive into the frigid New En-gland Atlantic, followed by a slow, easy swim beyond the surf. But in those first few days in Portland the anxieties of my actual social class take over. Educated middle-class profession-als never go careening half-cocked into the future, vulnerable to any surprise that might leap out at them. We always have a plan or at least a to-do list; we like to know that everything has been anticipated, that our lives are, in a sense, pre-lived. So what am I doing here, and in what order should I be doing it? I need a job and an apartment, but to get a job I need an address and a phone number and to get an apartment it helps to have evidence of stable employment. The only plan I can come up with is to do everything at once and hope that the teenagers at the Motel 6 switchboard can be trusted to serve as my answering machine.

The newspaper I pick up at the Clipper Mart bears the unexpected news that there are no apartments in Portland. Actually, there are plenty of condos and "executive apartments" for $1,000 a month or more, but the only low-rent options seem to be clustered in an area about a thirty-minute drive south, in the soothingly named town of Old Orchard Beach. Even there, though, the rents are right up at Key West levels— well over $500 for an efficiency. A few calls confirm my impression that winter housing for the poor consists of motel rooms that the more affluent fill up in the summer.[1] You get the low rates after Labor Day, and your lease expires in June. What about a share, then? Glenwood Apartments (not its real name) in Old Orchard Beach is advertising a room at $65 a week, share bath and kit with a woman described to me on the phone as "a character, but clean"—and I think, hey, that could be me or at least my new best friend. Navigating with my Clipper Mart map, I reach the declining, and evidently orchardless, beach town at about ten and am shown around Glenwood by Earl. He repeats the "character, but clean" part about my potential housemate, adding that they are "giving her a chance." I ask if she has a job, and, yes, she does cleaning. But I'll never meet her because the place is so disturbing, to the point of probably being illegal. We go into the basement of this ramshackle combination motel and boardinghouse, where Earl indicates a closed door—the kitchen, he says—but we can't go in now, because a guy is sleeping there. He chuckles, as if sleeping in kitchens is just another one of the eccentricities you have to put up with in the landlord business. So how do you cook? I want to know. Well, he isn't in there all the time. The room itself, just down the hall from the "kitchen," is half

---

[1] On Cape Cod, too, rising rents for apartments and houses are driving the working class into motels, where a room might go for $880 a month in winter but climbs to $1,440 a month in the tourist season. The *Cape Cod Times* describes families of four living squeezed into one room, cooking in microwaves, and eating on their beds (K. C. Myers, "Of Last Resort," *Cape Cod Times,* June 25, 2000).

the size of my little outpost in Motel 6 and contains two unmade twin beds, a two-drawer chest, a couple of lightbulbs on the ceiling, and nothing else. There is no window. Well, there is a windowlike structure near the ceiling, but it offers a view only of compacted dirt, such as one might normally see when looking up from the grave.

I walk back to the main street of town and set up my "office" at the pay phone near the pier, from which I secure invitations to view a few more apartments, forget the shares. At the SeaBreeze, I'm shown around by a large, contemptuous guy who tells me there are no problems here because he's a retired cop and his son-in-law is a cop too, and everyone knows this, but I can't tell whether I'm supposed to feel reassured or warned. Another putative plus: he keeps down the number of children in the place, and the ones that he gets don't make any trouble, you can take his word for that. But the rent is $150 a week, so it's on to the Biarritz, where a jolly gal shows me the efficiency for $110 a week—no TV, no linens, no dishware. What I don't like is the ground-floor part, right on a well-traveled commercial street, meaning you have a choice between privacy and light. Well, that's not all I don't like, but it's enough. I'm heading back to Portland in defeat when I notice that the Blue Haven Motel on Route 1 has apartments to rent, and the place looks so cute, in an Alpine sort of way, with its rows of tiny white cottages set against deep blue pines, that I stop. For $120 a week I can have a bed/living area with a kitchen growing off of it, linens included, and a TV that will have cable until the cable company notices that the former occupant is no longer paying the bill. Better yet, the security deposit is only $100, which I produce on the spot.

Given a few days or weeks more to look, maybe I could have done better. But the meter is running at the rate of $59 a day for my digs at the 6, which are resembling a Ballard creation more every day. On the afternoon of my third day there, I return to my room to find that the door no longer responds to my key. As it turns out, this is just management's way of drawing my attention to the fact that more money is due. It's a bad moment, though, lasting long enough for me to glimpse a future without toothbrush or change of clothes.

Now to find a job. I know from my Key West experience to apply for as many as possible, since a help-wanted ad may not mean that any help is wanted just now. Waitressing jobs aren't plentiful with the tourist season ending, and I'm looking for fresh challenges anyway. Clerical work is ruled out by wardrobe limitations. I don't have in my suitcase—or even in my closet back at home—enough office-type outfits to get me through a week. So I call about cleaning (both office and homes), warehouse and nursing home work, manufacturing, and a position called "general helper," which sounds friendly and altruistic. It's humbling, this business of applying for low-wage jobs, consisting as it does of offering yourself—your energy, your smile, your real or faked lifetime of experience—to a series of people for whom this is just not a very interesting package. At a tortilla factory, where my job would be to load dough balls onto a conveyor belt, the "interview" is completed by a bored secretary without so much as a "Hi, how are you?" I go to Goodwill, which I am curious about since I know from past research it has been positioning itself nationwide as the ideal employer for the postwelfare poor as well as the handicapped. I fill out the application and am told that the pay is $7 an hour and that someone will get back to me in about two weeks. During the entire transaction, which takes place in a warehouse where perhaps thirty people of both sexes are sorting through bins of used clothing, no one makes eye contact with me. Well, actually one person does. As I search for the exit, I notice a skinny, misshapen fellow standing on one foot with the other tucked behind his knee, staring at me balefully, his hands making swimming motions above his head, either for balance or to ward me off.

Not every place is so nonchalant. At a suburban Wal-Mart that is advertising a "job fair" I am seated at a table with some balloons attached to it (this is the "fair" part) to wait for Julie. She is flustered, when she shows up after about a ten-minute wait, because, as she explains, she just works on the floor and has never interviewed anyone before. Fortunately for her, the interview consists almost entirely of a four-page "opinion survey," with "no right or wrong answers," Julie assures me, just my own personal opinion in ten degrees from "totally agree" to "totally disagree."[2] As with the Winn-Dixie preemployment test I took in Key West, there are the usual questions about whether a coworker observed stealing should be forgiven or denounced, whether management is to blame if things go wrong, and if it's all right to be late when you have a "good excuse." The only thing that distinguishes this test is its obsession with marijuana, suggesting that it was authored by a serious stoner struggling to adjust to the corporate way of life. Among the propositions I am asked to opine about are, "Some

[2] Margaret Talbot reports in the *New York Times Magazine* that "personality testing in the workplace is at an all-time high" and now supports a $400-million-a-year industry (October 17, 1999, p. 28).

people work better when they're a little bit high," "Everyone tries marijuana," and, bafflingly, "Marijuana is the same as a drink." Hmm, what kind of drink? I want to ask. "The same" how—chemically or morally? Or should I write in something flippant like, "I wouldn't know because I don't drink"? The pay is $6.50, Julie tells me, but can shoot up to $7 pretty fast. She thinks I would be great in the ladies' department, and I tell her I think so too.

What these tests tell employers about potential employees is hard to imagine, since the "right" answers should be obvious to anyone who has ever encountered the principle of hierarchy and subordination. Do I work well with others? You bet, but never to the point where I would hesitate to inform on them for the slightest infraction. Am I capable of independent decision making? Oh yes, but I know better than to let this capacity interfere with a slavish obedience to orders. At The Maids, a housecleaning service, I am given something called the "Accutrac personality test," which warns at the beginning that "Accutrac has multiple measures which detect attempts to distort or 'psych out' the questionnaire." Naturally, I "never" find it hard "to stop moods of self-pity," nor do I imagine that others are talking about me behind my back or believe that "management and employees will always be in conflict because they have totally different sets of goals." The real function of these tests, I decide, is to convey information not to the employer but to the potential employee, and the information being conveyed is always: You will have no secrets from us. We don't just want your muscles and that portion of your brain that is directly connected to them, we want your innermost self.

The main thing I learn from the job-hunting process is that, despite all the help-wanted ads and job fairs, Portland is just another $6–$7-an-hour town. This should be as startling to economists as a burst of exotic radiation is to astronomers. If the supply (of labor) is low relative to demand, the price should rise, right? That is the "law." At one of the maid services I apply at—Merry Maids—my potential boss keeps me for an hour and fifteen minutes, most of which is spent listening to her complain about the difficulty of finding reliable help. It's easy enough to think of a solution, because she's offering "$200 to $250" a week for an average of forty hours' work. "Don't try to put that into dollars per hour," she warns, seeing my brow furrow as I tackle the not-very-long division. "We don't calculate it that way." I do, however, and $5 to $6 an hour for what this lady freely admits is heavy labor with a high risk of repetitive-stress injuries seems guaranteed to repel all mathematically able job seekers. But I am realizing that, just as in Key West, one job will never be enough. In the new version of the law of supply and demand, jobs are so cheap—as measured by the pay—that a worker is encouraged to take on as many of them as she possibly can.

After two days of sprinkling job applications throughout the greater Portland area, I force myself to sit in my room at the 6, where I am marooned until the Blue Haven will let me in on Sunday, and wait for the phone to ring. This takes more effort than you might think, because the room is too small for pacing and too dingy for daydreaming, should I have been calm enough to give that a try. Fortunately, the phone rings twice before noon, and—more out of claustrophobia than any serious economic calculation—I accept the first two jobs that are offered. A nursing home wants me on weekends for $7 an hour, starting tomorrow; The Maids is pleased to announce that I "passed" the Accutrac test and can start on Monday at

7:30 A.M. This is the friendliest and best-paying maid service I have encountered—$6.65 an hour, though as a punishment this will drop to $6 for two weeks if I fail to show up for a day.[3] I don't understand exactly what maid services do and how they are different from agencies, but Tammy, the office manager at The Maids, assures me that the work will be familiar and easy, since "cleaning is in our blood." I'm not so sure about the easy part after the warnings I got at Merry Maids, but I figure my back should be able to hold out for a week. We're supposed to be done at about 3:30 every day, which will leave plenty of time for job hunting on weekday afternoons. I have my eye on a potato chip factory a ten-minute drive from the Blue Haven, for example, or I can always search out L.L. Bean and fill catalog orders from what I hope will be an ergonomically congenial seat. This is beginning to look like a plan: from maids' service to something better, with the nursing home tiding me over during the transition. To celebrate, I eat dinner at Appleby's—a burger and a glass of red wine for $11.95 plus tip, consumed at the bar while involuntarily watching ESPN.

On my fourth full day in Portland, I get up at 4:45 to be sure to get to the Woodcrest Residential Facility (not its real name) for the start of my shift at 7:00. I am a dietary aide, which sounds important and technical, and at first the work seems agreeable enough. I get to wear my own clothes, meaning T-shirt and khakis or jeans, augmented only by the mandatory hairnet and an apron at my own discretion. I don't even have to bring lunch, since we get to eat anything left over after

[3] The Bureau of Labor Statistics found full-time "private household workers and servants" earning a median income of $223 a week in 1998, which is $23 a week below the poverty level for a family of three. For a forty-hour week, our pay at The Maids would amount to $266, or $43 above the poverty level.

the residents, as we respectfully call them, have eaten their share. Linda, my supervisor—a kindly-looking woman of about thirty—even takes time to brief me about my rights: I don't have to put up with any sexual harassment, particularly from Robert, even though he's the owner's son. Any problems and I'm to come straight to her, and I get the feeling she'd appreciate getting a Robert-related complaint now and then. On the other hand, there is severe discipline for screwups that could endanger lives, like when some of the teenage boys who work on weekends put butter pats in a light fixture and the melted butter leaked onto the floor, creating a hazardously slippery region—not that she expects that kind of thing from me. Today we will be working the locked Alzheimer's ward, bringing breakfast from the main kitchen downstairs to the smaller kitchen on the ward, serving the residents, cleaning up afterward, and then readying ourselves for their lunch.

For a former waitress such as myself, this is pretty much a breeze. The residents start drifting in forty minutes before breakfast is ready, by walker and wheelchair or just marching stiffly on their own power, and scuffle briefly over who sits where. I rush around pouring coffee—decaf only, Linda warns, otherwise things can get pretty wild—and taking "orders," trying to think of it as a restaurant, although in a normal restaurant, I cannot help thinking, very few customers smell like they're carrying a fresh dump in their undies. If someone rejects the French toast we're offering, Linda and I make toast or a peanut butter sandwich, because the idea, especially at breakfast, is to get them eating fast before they collapse into their plates from low blood sugar or escape back out into the corridor. There's a certain amount of running but no big worry about forgetting things—our "customers" aren't strong in the memory department themselves. I make an effort to learn names: Marguerite, who arrives in the dining room clutching a teddy bear and wearing nothing but a diaper below the waist; Grace, who tracks me with an accusing stare and demands that her cup be refilled even when it hasn't been touched; Letty, a diabetic who has to be watched because she sneaks doughnuts from other people's plates. Ruthie, who softens her French toast by pouring orange juice over it and much of the table, is one of the more with-it gals. She asks my name, and when I tell her, she hoots "Barbara Bush!" Despite my vigorous protestations, the joke is repeated twice during the breakfast service.

The ugly part is cleaning up. I hadn't realized that a dietary aide is, in large measure, a dishwasher, and there are about forty people—counting the nurses and CNAs (Certified Nursing Assistants) who have scrounged breakfasts with the residents—to clean up after. You scrape uneaten food off the dishes and into the disposal by hand, rinse the dishes, presoak them, stack them in a rack, and load the rack into the dishwashing machine, which involves bending down almost to floor level with the full rack, which I would guess at about fifteen to twenty pounds, held out in front of you. After the machine has run its course, you let the dishes cool enough to handle, unload the rack, and reload the dishwasher—all the while continuing to clear tables and fetch meals for stragglers. The trick is to always have a new rack ready to go into the machine the minute the last load is done. I've been washing dishes since I was six years old, when my mother assigned me that task so she could enjoy her postprandial cigarette in a timely fashion, and I kind of like working with water, but it's all I can do to keep up with the pace of the dishwashing machine on the one hand and the flow of dirty plates on the other. With the dishes under control, Linda has me vacuum the carpet in the dining room, which really doesn't do anything for the sticky patches, so there's a lot of climbing under tables and scratching mushed muffins off the floor with my fingernails.

At my midmorning break I join Pete, one of the two cooks on duty in the main kitchen, for a cigarette date. I had chatted with him when I first arrived at seven, before Linda showed up, and he had three questions for me: Where was I from? Where was I living now? Was I married? I give him the short answer to the last question, leaving out the boyfriend for the moment, partly because it doesn't make sense to talk about "the man I live with" when I'm not living with him just now and partly, I admit, because of a craven desire to recruit Pete as an ally, on whatever terms should present themselves. A dietary aide, as I understand the job, is as dependent on a cook as a waitress is. He or she can either make life relatively easy for a server or, if so disposed, set her up for a serious fall. So I go out to the parking lot with him and sit in his car smoking his Marlboros, which feels awkwardly like a real date except that the car doors are wide open to let out the smoke. How do I like the place? Just fine, I tell him, and since my dad ended his days in an Alzheimer's facility I feel almost at home—which is, creepily enough, the truth. Well, watch out for Molly, he warns me. She's good to work with but she'll stab you in the back. Linda's OK but she came down hard on Pete last week for letting a dessert slip onto a diabetic's tray (residents who can't make it to the dining room have trays made up for them in the kitchen), and what does she think this is, a goddamn hospital? Look, nobody gets out of here alive. Watch out for Leon too, who has a habit of following his female coworkers into service closets.

In fact, watch out for everyone, because the place feeds on gossip and whatever you say will be public knowledge in a matter of hours. And what do I do for excitement? "Oh, read," I tell him. No drinking or carousing? I shake my head primly, feeling like a real goody-goody or at least a barren subject for the gossips, present company included.

I should make it clear that we're not talking about boyfriend material here. Pete is probably ten years my junior (though he doesn't seem to realize that and I see no reason to point it out) and, despite a striking resemblance to a currently popular comic actor, has no evident sense of humor. If his story is to be believed, he's as much an impostor as I am (though of course he doesn't know that either). See, he makes only $7 an hour himself, he tells me, though he's made a hell of a lot more in restaurants, but it doesn't bother him, on account of some big gambling wins a few years ago and clever investments since. If he's so rich, I can't help wondering, then why is he driving this rusty old wreck and how come his front teeth are so scraggly and sparse? And what is a self-respecting restaurant cook doing in this flavor-free environment anyway, where a third to a half of the meals get pureed as soon as they're prepared? But of course the question I ask is different: So why work at all if you have so much money? Oh, he tried staying home, but you get stir-crazy, you know, you start feeling like an outcast. And this touches me, somehow, even more than the presumptive lie about his assets: that this place he has described as so morbidly dysfunctional could amount to a real and compelling human community. Would I maybe like to go for a walk on the beach someday after work? Yeah, OK—and I bound back to brace myself for lunch.

Surprisingly, a number of the more sentient residents seem

to recognize me at the lunch service. One of them grips my arm when I bring her ham steak, whispering, "You're a good person, you know that?" and repeats the accolade with each item I deliver. Another resident tells me I'm looking "gorgeous," and one of the RNs actually remembers my name. This could work, I am thinking, I will become a luminous beacon in the gathering darkness of dementia, compensating, in some cosmic system of justice, for the impersonal care my father received in a far less loving facility. I happily fill special requests for ice cream and grilled cheese sandwiches; I laugh at the Barbara Bush joke when it comes up again, and again. The saintly mood lasts until I refill the milk glass of a tiny, scabrous old lady with wild white hair who looks like she's been folded into her wheelchair and squished. "I want to throw you," she seems to be saying, and when I bend down to confirm this improbable aspiration, the old fiend throws the entire glass at me, soaking my khakis from groin to ankle. "Ha ha," my erstwhile admirers cackle, "she wet her pants!" But at least I am no longer an outcast, as Pete would say, in this strange white state. I have been inducted into a world rich with gossip and intrigue, and now baptized in the whitest of fluids.

Saturday, my last night at the 6, and I refuse to spend it crushed in my room. But what is a person of limited means and no taste for "carousing" to do? Several times during the week, I have driven past the "Deliverance" church downtown, and the name alone exerts a scary attraction. Could there really be a whole congregation of people who have never heard of the James Dickey novel and subsequent movie? Or, worse yet, is this band of Christians thoroughly familiar with that story of homosexual rape in the woods? The marquee in front of the church is advertising a Saturday night "tent revival," which sounds like the perfect entertainment for an atheist out on her own. I drive through a menacing area filled with deserted warehouses—Dickey, be gone!—until the tent comes looming up out of the dusk. Unfortunately, from an entertainment point of view, only about sixty of the approximately three hundred folding chairs are populated. I count three or four people of color—African and, I would guess, Mexican Americans; everyone else is a tragic-looking hillbilly type, my very own people, genetically speaking (Ehrenreich is a name acquired through marriage; my maiden name, Alexander, derives directly from Kentucky).

I chat with a woman sitting near me—"Nice night," "You come from far?" and things like that—and she lends me her Bible since I seem to be the only one present without a personal copy. It's a relief when one of the ten or so men on the stage orders us to stand and start singing, because the folding chair is torturing my overworked back. I even join in the rhythmic clapping and swaying, which seems to define a minimal level of participation. There are a few genuine adepts present who throw themselves rapturously into the music, eyes shut, arms upraised, waiting, no doubt, for the onset of glossolalia.

But before anything interesting can happen, the preaching commences. A man in shirtsleeves tells us what a marvelous book the Bible is and bemoans the fact that people buy so many inferior books when you really need just the one. Someone on TV tells you to read some (secular) book and then "it goes up, you know—what's the word?" I think *sales* is the word he wants but no one can figure out how to help him. Anyway, "it" could be three hundred, and then it's a ratio of ten to one. Huh? Next a Mexican American fellow takes over the mike, shuts his eyes tight, and delivers a rapid-fire summary of our debt to the crucified Christ. Then it's an older white guy attacking "this wicked city" for its heretically inadequate contribution of souls to the revival—which costs money, you know, this tent didn't just put itself up. We're talking overhead, he goes on, not someone making money for themselves, and when you consider what Jesus gave so that we could enjoy eternal life with him in Heaven . . .

I can't help letting my mind wander to the implications of Alzheimer's disease for the theory of an immortal soul. Who wants an afterlife if the immediate pre-afterlife is spent clutching the arms of a wheelchair, head bent back at a forty-five-degree angle, eyes and mouth wide open and equally mute, like so many of my charges at the Woodcrest? Is the "soul" that lives forever the one we possess at the moment of death, in which case heaven must look something like the Woodcrest, with plenty of CNAs and dietary aides to take care of those who died in a state of mental decomposition? Or is it our personally best soul—say, the one that indwells in us at the height of our cognitive powers and moral aspirations? In which case, it can't possibly matter whether demented diabetics eat cupcakes or not, because from a purely soteriological standpoint, they're already dead.

The preaching goes on, interrupted with dutiful "amens." It would be nice if someone would read this sad-eyed crowd the Sermon on the Mount, accompanied by a rousing commentary on income inequality and the need for a hike in the minimum wage. But Jesus makes his appearance here only as a corpse; the living man, the wine-guzzling vagrant and precocious socialist, is never once mentioned, nor anything he ever had to say. Christ crucified rules, and it may be that the true business of modern Christianity is to crucify him again and again so that he can never get a word out of his mouth. I would like to stay around for the speaking in tongues, should it occur, but the mosquitoes, worked into a frenzy by all this talk of His blood, are launching a full-scale attack. I get up to leave, timing my exit for when the preacher's metronomic head movements have him looking the other way, and walk out to search for my car, half expecting to find Jesus out there in the dark, gagged and tethered to a tent pole.

SUNDAY I AT LAST MOVE INTO THE BLUE HAVEN, SO PLEASED TO BE out of the 6 that the shortcomings of my new home seem minor, even, at first, endearing. It's smaller than I had recalled, for one thing, since a toolshed used by the motel owners takes up part of my cottage space, and this leads to a certain unfortunate blending of the biological functions. With the toilet less than four feet from the tiny kitchen table, I have to close the bathroom door or I feel like I'm eating in a latrine, and the fact that the head of the bed is about seven feet from the stove means that the flounder I fry up for my housewarming dinner lingers all night. Frying is pretty much all I can do, since the kitchen equipment is limited to a frying pan, a plate, a small bowl, a coffeemaker, and one large drinking glass—without even a proverbial pot to pee in. The idea is improvisation: the foil containers that come from salad bars can be reused as dishes; the lone plate becomes a cutting board. The concavity in the center of the bed is rectified by sleeping on a folded-up towel, and so forth. Not to worry—I have an address, two jobs, and a Rent-A-Wreck. The anxiety that gripped me those first few days at the 6 is finally beginning to ebb.

As it turns out, the mere fact of having a unit to myself makes me an aristocrat within the Blue Haven community. The other long-term residents, whom I encounter at the communal laundry shed, are blue-collar people with uniforms and overalls to wash, and generally quiet at night. Mostly they are couples with children, much like the white working-class people occasionally glimpsed on sitcoms, only, unlike their TV counterparts, my neighbors are crowded three or four into an efficiency, or at most a one-bedroom, apartment. One young guy asks which unit I'm in and then tells me he used to live in that very same one himself—along with two friends. A middle-aged woman with a three-year-old granddaughter in tow tells me, in a comforting tone, that it is always hard at the beginning, living in a motel, especially if you're used to a house, but you adjust after a while, you put it out of your mind. She, for example, has been at the Blue Haven for eleven years now.

I am rested and ready for anything when I arrive at The Maids' office suite Monday at 7:30 A.M. I know nothing about cleaning services like this one, which, according to the brochure I am given, has over three hundred franchises nationwide, and most of what I know about domestics in general comes from nineteenth-century British novels and *Upstairs, Downstairs*.[4] Prophetically enough, I caught a rerun of that

---

[4] Nationwide and even international cleaning services like Merry Maids, Molly Maids, and The Maids International, all of which have arisen since the seventies, now control 20–25 percent of the housecleaning business. In a 1997 article about Merry Maids, *Franchise Times* reported tersely that "category is booming, niche is hot too, as Americans look to outsource work even at home" ("72 Merry Maids," *Franchise Times,* December 1997). Not all cleaning services do well, with a high rate of failure among the informal, mom-and-pop services, like the one I applied to by phone that did not even require a cursory interview—all I had to do was show up at seven the next morning. The "boom" is

very show on PBS over the weekend and was struck by how terribly correct the servants looked in their black-and-white uniforms and how much wiser they were than their callow, egotistical masters. We too have uniforms, though they are more oafish than dignified—ill-fitting and in an overloud combination of kelly-green pants and a blinding sunflower-yellow polo shirt. And, as is explained in writing and over the next day and a half of training, we too have a special code of decorum. No smoking anywhere, or at least not within fifteen minutes of arrival at a house. No drinking, eating, or gum chewing in a house. No cursing in a house, even if the owner is not present, and—perhaps to keep us in practice—no obscenities even in the office. So this is Downstairs, is my chirpy first thought. But I have no idea, of course, just how far down these stairs will take me.

Forty minutes go by before anyone acknowledges my presence with more than a harried nod. During this time the other employees arrive, about twenty of them, already glowing in their uniforms, and breakfast on the free coffee, bagels, and doughnuts The Maids kindly provides for us. All but one of the others are female, with an average age I would guess in the late twenties, though the range seems to go from prom-fresh to well into the Medicare years. There is a pleasant sort of bustle as people get their breakfasts and fill plastic buckets with rags

concentrated among the national and international chains—outfits like Merry Maids, Molly Maids, Mini Maids, Maid Brigade, and The Maids International—all named, curiously enough, to highlight the more antique aspects of the industry, although the "maid" may occasionally be male. Merry Maids claimed to be growing at 15–20 percent a year in 1996, while spokesmen for Molly Maids and The Maids International each told me in interviews conducted after I left Maine that their firms' sales are growing by 25 percent a year.

and bottles of cleaning fluids, but surprisingly little conversation outside of a few references to what people ate (pizza) and drank (Jell-O shots are mentioned) over the weekend. Since the room in which we gather contains only two folding chairs, both of them occupied, the other new girl and I sit cross-legged on the floor, silent and alert, while the regulars get sorted into teams of three or four and dispatched to the day's list of houses. One of the women explains to me that teams do not necessarily return to the same houses week after week, nor do you have any guarantee of being on the same team from one day to the next. This, I suppose, is one of the advantages of a corporate cleaning service to its customers: there are no sticky and possibly guilt-ridden relationships involved, because the customers communicate almost entirely with Tammy, the office manager, or with Ted, the franchise owner and our boss.[5] The advantage to the cleaning person is harder to determine, since the pay compares so poorly to what an independent cleaner is likely to earn—up to $15 an hour, I've heard. While I wait in the inner room, where the phone is and Tammy has her desk, to be issued a uniform, I hear her tell a potential customer on the phone that The Maids charges $25 per person-hour. The company gets $25 and we get $6.65 for each hour we work? I think I must have misheard, but a few minutes later I hear her say the same thing to another inquirer. So the only advantage of working here as opposed to freelancing is that you don't need a

[5] The maids' wages, their Social Security taxes, their green cards, backaches, and child care problems—all these are the sole concern of the company, meaning the local franchise owner. If there are complaints on either side, they are addressed to the franchise owner; the customer and the actual workers need never interact. Since the franchise owner is usually a middle-class white person, cleaning services are the ideal solution for anyone still sensitive enough to find the traditional employer-maid relationship morally vexing.

clientele or even a car. You can arrive straight from welfare or, in my case, the bus station—fresh off the boat.[6]

At last, after all the other employees have sped off in the company's eye-catching green-and-yellow cars, I am led into a tiny closet-sized room off the inner office to learn my trade via videotape. The manager at another maid service where I'd applied had told me she didn't like to hire people who had done cleaning before because they were resistant to learning the company's system, so I prepare to empty my mind of all prior housecleaning experience. There are four tapes—dusting, bathrooms, kitchen, and vacuuming—each starring an attractive, possibly Hispanic young woman who moves about serenely in obedience to the male voiceover: For vacuuming, begin in the master bedroom; when dusting, begin with the room directly off the kitchen. When you enter a room, mentally divide it into sections no wider than your reach. Begin in the section to your left and, within each section, move from left to right and top to bottom. This way nothing is ever overlooked.

I like *Dusting* best, for its undeniable logic and a certain kind of austere beauty. When you enter a house, you spray a white rag with Windex and place it in the left pocket of your green apron. Another rag, sprayed with disinfectant, goes into the middle pocket, and a yellow rag bearing wood polish in the right-hand pocket. A dry rag, for buffing surfaces, occupies the right-hand pocket of your slacks. Shiny surfaces get Windexed, wood gets wood polish, and everything else is wiped dust-free

[6] I don't know what proportion of my fellow workers at The Maids in Portland had been on welfare, but the owner of The Maids' franchise in Andover, Massachusetts, told me in a phone interview that half his employees are former welfare recipients and that they are as reliable as anyone else.

with disinfectant. Every now and then Ted pops in to watch with me, pausing the video to underscore a particularly dramatic moment: "See how she's working around the vase? That's an accident waiting to happen." If Ted himself were in a video, it would have to be a cartoon, because the only features sketched onto his pudgy face are brown buttonlike eyes and a tiny pug nose; his belly, encased in a polo shirt, overhangs the waistline of his shorts. "You know, all this was figured out with a stopwatch," he tells me with something like pride. When the video warns against oversoaking our rags with cleaning fluids, he pauses it to tell me there's a danger in undersoaking too, especially if it's going to slow me down. "Cleaning fluids are less expensive than your time." It's good to know that *something* is cheaper than my time, or that in the hierarchy of the company's values I rank above Windex.

Vacuuming is the most disturbing video, actually a double feature beginning with an introduction to the special backpack vacuum we are to use. Yes, the vacuum cleaner actually straps onto your back, a chubby fellow who introduces himself as its inventor explains. He suits up, pulling the straps tight across and under his chest and then says proudly into the camera: "See, I *am* the vacuum cleaner." It weighs only ten pounds, he claims, although, as I soon find out, with the attachments dangling from the strap around your waist, the total is probably more like fourteen. What about my petulant and much-pampered lower back? The inventor returns to the theme of human/ machine merger: when properly strapped in, we too will be vacuum cleaners, constrained only by the cord that attaches us to an electrical outlet, and vacuum cleaners don't have backaches. Somehow all this information exhausts me, and I watch the second video, which explains the actual procedures for vacuuming, with the detached interest of a cineast. Could the model maid be an actual maid and the model home someone's actual dwelling? And who are these people whose idea of decorating is matched pictures of mallard ducks in flight and whose house is perfectly characterless and pristine even before the model maid sets to work?

At first I find the videos on kitchens and bathrooms baffling, and it takes me several minutes to realize why: there is no *water,* or almost no water, involved. I was taught to clean by my mother, a compulsive housekeeper who employed water so hot you needed rubber gloves to get into it and in such Niagara-like quantities that most microbes were probably crushed by the force of it before the soap suds had a chance to rupture their cell walls. But germs are never mentioned in the videos provided by The Maids. Our antagonists exist entirely in the visible world—soap scum, dust, counter crud, dog hair, stains, and smears—and are to be attacked by damp rag or, in hard-core cases, by Dobie (the brand of plastic scouring pad we use). We scrub only to remove impurities that might be detectable to a customer by hand or by eye; otherwise our only job is to wipe. Nothing is said about the possibility of transporting bacteria, by rag or by hand, from bathroom to kitchen or even from one house to the next. It is the "cosmetic touches" that the videos emphasize and that Ted, when he wanders back into the room, continually directs my eye to. Fluff up all throw pillows and arrange them symmetrically. Brighten up stainless steel sinks with baby oil. Leave all spice jars, shampoos, etc., with their labels facing outward. Comb out the fringes of Persian carpets with a pick. Use the vacuum cleaner to create a special, fernlike pattern in the carpets. The loose ends of toilet paper and paper towel rolls have to be given a special fold (the same one you'll find in hotel bathrooms). "Messes" of loose paper, clothing, or toys are to be stacked into "neat messes." Finally, the house is to be sprayed with the cleaning service's signature floral-scented air freshener, which will signal to the owners, the moment they return home, that, yes, their house has been "cleaned."[7]

After a day's training I am judged fit to go out with a team, where I soon discover that life is nothing like the movies, at least not if the movie is *Dusting*. For one thing, compared with our actual pace, the training videos were all in slow motion. We do not walk to the cars with our buckets full of cleaning fluids and utensils in the morning, we run, and when we pull up to a house, we run with our buckets to the door. Liza, a good-

---

[7] When I described the methods employed by The Maids to housecleaning expert Cheryl Mendelson, author of *Home Comforts,* she was incredulous. A rag moistened with disinfectant will not get a countertop clean, she told me, because most disinfectants are inactivated by contact with organic matter—i.e., dirt—so their effectiveness declines with each swipe of the rag. What you need is a detergent and hot water, followed by a rinse. As for floors, she judged the amount of water we used—one half of a small bucket, which was never any warmer than room temperature—to be grossly inadequate, and, in fact, the water I wiped around on floors was often an unsavory gray. I also ran The Maids' cleaning methods by Don Aslett, author of numerous books on cleaning techniques and self-styled "number one cleaner in America." He was hesitant to criticize The Maids directly, perhaps because he is, or told me he is, a frequent speaker at conventions of cleaning service franchise holders, but he did tell me how he would clean a countertop. First, spray it thoroughly with an all-purpose cleaner, then let it sit for three to four minutes of "kill time," and finally wipe dry with a clean cloth. Merely wiping the surface with a damp cloth, he said, just spreads the dirt around. But the point at The Maids, apparently, is not to clean so much as to create the appearance of *having been cleaned,* not to sanitize but to create a kind of stage setting for family life. And the stage setting Americans seem to prefer is sterile only in the metaphorical sense, like a motel room or the fake interiors in which soap operas and sitcoms take place.

natured woman in her thirties who is my first team leader,
explains that we are given only so many minutes per house,
ranging from under sixty for a 1½-bathroom apartment to
two hundred or more for a multibathroom "first timer." I'd
like to know why anybody worries about Ted's time limits
if we're being paid by the hour but hesitate to display anything that might be interpreted as attitude. As we get to each
house, Liza assigns our tasks, and I cross my fingers to ward off
bathrooms and vacuuming. Even dusting, though, gets aerobic
under pressure, and after about an hour of it—reaching to get
door tops, crawling along floors to wipe baseboards, standing
on my bucket to attack the higher shelves—I wouldn't mind
sitting down with a tall glass of water. But as soon as you complete your assigned task, you report to the team leader to be
assigned to help someone else. Once or twice, when the normal
process of evaporation is deemed too slow, I am assigned to
dry a scrubbed floor by putting rags under my feet and skating
around on it. Usually, by the time I get out to the car and am
dumping the dirty water used on floors and wringing out rags,
the rest of the team is already in the car with the motor running. Liza assures me that they've never left anyone behind at a
house, not even, presumably, a very new person whom nobody
knows.

In my interview, I had been promised a thirty-minute lunch
break, but this turns out to be a five-minute pit stop at a convenience store, if that. I bring my own sandwich—the same
turkey breast and cheese every day—as do a couple of the others; the rest eat convenience store fare, a bagel or doughnut
salvaged from our free breakfast, or nothing at all. The two
older married women I'm teamed up with eat best—sandwiches

and fruit. Among the younger women, lunch consists of a slice of pizza, a "pizza pocket" (a roll of dough surrounding some pizza sauce), or a small bag of chips. Bear in mind we are not office workers, sitting around idling at the basal metabolic rate. A poster on the wall in the office cheerily displays the number of calories burned per minute at our various tasks, ranging from about 3.5 for dusting to 7 for vacuuming. If you assume an average of 5 calories per minute in a seven-hour day (eight hours minus time for travel between houses), you need to be taking in 2,100 calories in addition to the resting minimum of, say, 900 or so. I get pushy with Rosalie, who is new like me and fresh from high school in a rural northern part of the state, about the meagerness of her lunches, which consist solely of Doritos—a half bag from the day before or a freshly purchased small-sized bag. She just didn't have anything in the house, she says (though she lives with her boyfriend and his mother), and she certainly doesn't have any money to buy lunch, as I find out when I offer to fetch her a soda from a Quik Mart and she has to admit she doesn't have eighty-nine cents. I treat her to the soda, wishing I could force her, mommylike, to take milk instead. So how does she hold up for an eight- or even nine-hour day? "Well," she concedes, "I get dizzy sometimes."

How poor are they, my coworkers? The fact that anyone is working this job at all can be taken as prima facie evidence of some kind of desperation or at least a history of mistakes and disappointments, but it's not for me to ask. In the prison movies that provide me with a mental guide to comportment, the new guy doesn't go around shaking hands and asking, "Hi there, what are you in for?" So I listen, in the cars and when we're assembled in the office, and learn, first, that no one seems to be homeless. Almost everyone is embedded in extended families or families artificially extended with house-mates. People talk about visiting grandparents in the hospital or sending birthday cards to a niece's husband; single mothers live with their own mothers or share apartments with a coworker or boyfriend. Pauline, the oldest of us, owns her own home, but she sleeps on the living room sofa, while her four grown children and three grandchildren fill up the bedrooms.[8]

But although no one, apparently, is sleeping in a car, there are signs, even at the beginning, of real difficulty if not actual misery. Half-smoked cigarettes are returned to the pack. There

---

[8] The women I worked with were all white and, with one exception, Anglo, as are the plurality of housecleaners in America, or at least those known to the Bureau of Labor Statistics. Of the "private household cleaners and servants" it managed to locate in 1998, the BLS reports that 36.8 percent were Hispanic, 15.8 percent black, and 2.7 percent "other." However, the association between housecleaning and minority status is well established in the psyches of the white employing class. When my daughter, Rosa, was introduced to the father of a wealthy Harvard classmate, he ventured that she must have been named for a favorite maid. And Audre Lorde reported an experience she had in 1967: "I wheel my two-year-old daughter in a shopping cart through a super-market . . . and a little white girl riding past in her mother's cart calls out excit-edly, 'Oh look, Mommy, a baby maid'" (quoted in Mary Romero, *Maid in the U.S.A.: Perspectives on Gender* [New York: Routledge, 1992], p. 72). But the composition of the household workforce is hardly fixed and has changed with the life chances of the different ethnic groups. In the late nineteenth cen-tury, Irish and German immigrants served the urban upper and middle classes, then left for the factories as soon as they could. Black women replaced them, accounting for 60 percent of all domestics in the 1940s, and dominated the field until other occupations began to open up to them. Similarly, West Coast maids were disproportionately Japanese American until that group too found more congenial options (see Phyllis Palmer, *Domesticity and Dirt: Housewives and Domestic Servants in the United States, 1920–1945* [Temple University Press, 1989], pp. 12–13). Today, the color of the hand that pushes the sponge varies from region to region: Chicanas in the Southwest, Caribbeans in New York, native Hawaiians in Hawaii, native whites, many of recent rural extrac-tion, in the Midwest and, of course, Maine.

are discussions about who will come up with fifty cents for a toll and whether Ted can be counted on for prompt reimbursement. One of my teammates gets frantic about a painfully impacted wisdom tooth and keeps making calls from our houses to try to locate a source of free dental care. When my— or, I should say, Liza's—team discovers there is not a single Dobie in our buckets, I suggest that we stop at a convenience store and buy one rather than drive all the way back to the office. But it turns out I haven't brought any money with me and we cannot put together $2 between the four of us.

The Friday of my first week at The Maids is unnaturally hot for Maine in early September—95 degrees, according to the digital time-and-temperature displays offered by banks that we pass. I'm teamed up with the sad-faced Rosalie and our leader, Maddy, whose sullenness, under the circumstances, is almost a relief after Liza's relentless good cheer. Liza, I've learned, is the highest-ranking cleaner, a sort of supervisor really, and said to be something of a snitch, but Maddy, a single mom of maybe twenty-seven or so, has worked for only three months and broods about her child care problems. Her boyfriend's sister, she tells me on the drive to our first house, watches her eighteen-month-old for $50 a week, which is a stretch on The Maids' pay, plus she doesn't entirely trust the sister, but a real day care center could be as much as $90 a week. After polishing off the first house, no problem, we grab "lunch"— Doritos for Rosalie and a bag of Pepperidge Farm Goldfish for Maddy—and head out into the exurbs for what our instruction sheet warns is a five-bathroom spread and a first-timer to boot. Still, the size of the place makes us pause for a moment, buckets in hand, before searching out an appropriately humble entrance.[9] It sits there like a beached ocean liner, the prow cutting through swells of green turf, windows without number. "Well, well," Maddy says, reading the owner's name from our instruction sheet, "Mrs. W. and her big-ass house. I hope she's going to give us lunch."

Mrs. W. is not in fact happy to see us, grimacing with exasperation when the black nanny ushers us into the family room or sunroom or den or whatever kind of specialized space she is sitting in. After all, she already has the nanny, a cooklike person, and a crew of men doing some sort of finishing touches on the construction to supervise. No, she doesn't want to take us around the house, because she already explained everything to the office on the phone, but Maddy stands there, with Rosalie and me behind her, until she relents. We are to move everything on all surfaces, she instructs during the tour, and get underneath and be sure to do every bit of the several miles, I calculate, of baseboards. And be mindful of the baby, who's napping and can't have cleaning fluids of any kind near her.

Then I am let loose to dust. In a situation like this, where I don't even know how to name the various kinds of rooms, The Maids' special system turns out to be a lifesaver. All I have to

[9] For the affluent, houses have been swelling with no apparent limit. The square footage of new homes increased by 39 percent between 1971 and 1996, to include "family rooms," home entertainment rooms, home offices, bedrooms, and often a bathroom for each family member ("Détente in the Housework Wars," *Toronto Star,* November 20, 1999). By the second quarter of 1999, 17 percent of new homes were larger than three thousand square feet, which is usually considered the size threshold for household help, or the point at which a house becomes unmanageable to the people who live in it ("Molding Loyal Pamperers for the Newly Rich," *New York Times,* October 24, 1999).

do is keep moving from left to right, within rooms and between rooms, trying to identify landmarks so I don't accidentally do a room or a hallway twice. Dusters get the most complete biographical overview, due to the necessity of lifting each object and tchotchke individually, and I learn that Mrs. W. is an alumna of an important women's college, now occupying herself by monitoring her investments and the baby's bowel movements. I find special charts for this latter purpose, with spaces for time of day, most recent fluid intake, consistency, and color. In the master bedroom, I dust a whole shelf of books on pregnancy, breastfeeding, the first six months, the first year, the first two years—and I wonder what the child care–deprived Maddy makes of all this. Maybe there's been some secret division of the world's women into breeders and drones, and those at the maid level are no longer supposed to be reproducing at all. Maybe this is why our office manager, Tammy, who was once a maid herself, wears inch-long fake nails and tarty little outfits— to show she's advanced to the breeder caste and can't be sent out to clean anymore.

It is hotter inside than out, un-air-conditioned for the benefit of the baby, I suppose, but I do all right until I encounter the banks of glass doors that line the side and back of the ground floor. Each one has to be Windexed, wiped, and buffed— inside and out, top to bottom, left to right, until it's as streakless and invisible as a material substance can be. Outside, I can see the construction guys knocking back Gatorade, but the rule is that no fluid or food item can touch a maid's lips when she's inside a house. Now, sweat, even in unseemly quantities, is nothing new to me. I live in a subtropical area where even the inactive can expect to be moist nine months out of the year. I work out, too, in my normal life and take a certain macho pride

in the *V*s of sweat that form on my T-shirt after ten minutes or
more on the StairMaster. But in normal life fluids lost are
immediately replaced. Everyone in yuppie-land—airports, for
example—looks like a nursing baby these days, inseparable
from their plastic bottles of water. Here, however, I sweat without replacement or pause, not in individual drops but in
continuous sheets of fluid soaking through my polo shirt,
pouring down the backs of my legs. The eyeliner I put on in the
morning—vain twit that I am—has long since streaked down
onto my cheeks, and I could wring my braid out if I wanted to.
Working my way through the living room(s), I wonder if Mrs.
W. will ever have occasion to realize that every single doodad
and *objet* through which she expresses her unique, individual
self is, from another vantage point, only an obstacle between
some thirsty person and a glass of water.

When I can find no more surfaces to wipe and have finally
exhausted the supply of rooms, Maddy assigns me to do the
kitchen floor. OK, except that Mrs. W. is *in* the kitchen, so I
have to go down on my hands and knees practically at her feet.
No, we don't have sponge mops like the one I use in my own
house; the hands-and-knees approach is a definite selling point
for corporate cleaning services like The Maids. "We clean floors
the old-fashioned way—*on our hands and knees*" (emphasis
added), the brochure for a competing firm boasts. In fact,
whatever advantages there may be to the hands-and-knees
approach—you're closer to your work, of course, and less
likely to miss a grimy patch—are undermined by the artificial
drought imposed by The Maids' cleaning system. We are
instructed to use less than half a small bucket of lukewarm
water for a kitchen and all adjacent scrubbable floors (breakfast nooks and other dining areas), meaning that within a few

minutes we are doing nothing more than redistributing the dirt evenly around the floor. There are occasional customer complaints about the cleanliness of our floors—for example, from a man who wiped up a spill on his freshly "cleaned" floor only to find the paper towel he employed for this purpose had turned gray. A mop and a full bucket of hot soapy water would not only get a floor cleaner but would be a lot more dignified for the person who does the cleaning. But it is this primal posture of submission—and of what is ultimately anal accessibility— that seems to gratify the consumers of maid services.[10]

I don't know, but Mrs. W.'s floor is hard—stone, I think, or at least a stonelike substance—and we have no knee pads with us today. I had thought in my middle-class innocence that knee pads were one of Monica Lewinsky's prurient fantasies, but no, they actually exist, and they're usually a standard part of our equipment. So here I am on my knees, working my way around the room like some fanatical penitent crawling through the stations of the cross, when I realize that Mrs. W. is staring at me fixedly—so fixedly that I am gripped for a moment by the wild possibility that I may have once given a lecture at her alma mater and she's trying to figure out where she's seen me before. If I were recognized, would I be fired? Would she at least be inspired to offer me a drink of water? Because I have decided that if water is actually offered, I'm taking it, rules or no rules, and if word of this infraction gets back to Ted, I'll just say I thought it would be rude to refuse. Not to worry, though. She's just watching that I don't leave out some stray square inch, and

---

[10] In *Home Comforts: The Art and Science of Keeping House* (Scribner, 1999), Cheryl Mendelson writes, "Never ask hired housecleaners to clean your floors on their hands and knees; the request is likely to be regarded as degrading" (p. 501).

when I rise painfully to my feet again, blinking through the sweat, she says, "Could you just scrub the floor in the entryway while you're at it?"

I rush home to the Blue Haven at the end of the day, pull down the blinds for privacy, strip off my uniform in the kitchen—the bathroom being too small for both a person and her discarded clothes—and stand in the shower for a good ten minutes, thinking all this water is *mine*. I have paid for it, in fact, I have earned it. I have gotten through a week at The Maids without mishap, injury, or insurrection. My back feels fine, meaning I'm not feeling it at all; even my wrists, damaged by carpal tunnel syndrome years ago, are issuing no complaints. Coworkers warned me that the first time they donned the backpack vacuum they felt faint, but not me. I am strong and I am, more than that, good. Did I toss my bucket of filthy water onto Mrs. W.'s casual white summer outfit? No. Did I take the wand of my vacuum cleaner and smash someone's Chinese porcelain statues or Hummel figurines? Not once. I was at all times cheerful, energetic, helpful, and as competent as a new hire can be expected to be. If I can do one week, I can do another, and might as well, since there's never been a moment for job-hunting. The 3:30 quitting time turns out to be a myth; often we don't return to the office until 4:30 or 5:00. And what did I think? That I was going to go out to interviews in my soaked and stinky postwork condition? I decide to reward myself with a sunset walk on Old Orchard Beach.

On account of the heat, there are still a few actual bathers on the beach, but I am content to sit in shorts and T-shirt and watch the ocean pummel the sand. When the sun goes down I walk back into the town to find my car and am amazed to hear a sound I associate with cities like New York and Berlin. There's a couple of Peruvian musicians playing in the little grassy island in the street near the pier, and maybe fifty people—locals and vacationers—have gathered around, offering their bland end-of-summer faces to the sound. I edge my way through the crowd and find a seat where I can see the musicians up close—the beautiful young guitarist and the taller man playing the flute. What are they doing in this rinky-dink blue-collar resort, and what does the audience make of this surprise visit from the dark-skinned South? The melody the flute lays out over the percussion is both utterly strange and completely familiar, as if it had been imprinted in the minds of my own peasant ancestors centuries ago and forgotten until this very moment. Everyone else seems to be as transfixed as I am. The musicians wink and smile at each other as they play, and I see then that they are the secret emissaries of a worldwide lower-class conspiracy to snatch joy out of degradation and filth. When the song ends, I give them a dollar, the equivalent of about ten minutes of sweat.

THE SUPERWOMAN MOOD DOES NOT LAST. FOR ONE THING, WHILE the muscles and joints are doing just fine, the skin has decided to rebel. At first I think the itchy pink bumps on my arms and legs must be poison ivy picked up at a lockout. Sometimes an owner forgets we are coming or forgets to leave a key under the mat or changes his or her mind about the service without thinking to notify Ted. This is not, for us, an occasion for joy like a snow day for the grade-school crowd, because Ted blames us for his customers' fecklessness. When owners forget we are coming, he explains at one of our morning send-off meetings, it "means something," like that they're dissatisfied and too passive-aggressive to tell us. Once, when I am with Pauline as my team leader, she calls Ted to report a lockout and his response, she reports ruefully, is, "Don't do this to me." So before we give up and declare a place a lockout, we search like cat burglars for alternative points of entry, which can mean trampling through overgrowth to peer into windows and test all the doors. I haven't seen any poison ivy, but who knows what other members of the poison family (oak, sumac, etc.) lurk in the flora of Maine?

Or maybe the cleaning fluids are at fault, except that then the rash should have begun on my hands. After two days of minor irritation, a full-scale epidermal breakdown is under way. I cover myself with anti-itch cream from Rite Aid but can manage to sleep only for an hour and a half at a time before the torment resumes. I wake up realizing I can work but probably shouldn't, if only because I look like a leper. Ted doesn't have much sympathy for illness, though; one of our morning meetings was on the subject of "working through it." Somebody, and he wasn't going to name names, he told us, was out with a migraine. "Now if I get a migraine I just pop two Excedrins and get on with my life. That's what you have to do—work through it." So it's in the spirit of a scientific experiment that I present myself at the office, wondering if my speckled and inflamed appearance will be enough to get me sent home. Certainly I wouldn't want anyone who looks like me handling my children's toys or bars of bathroom soap. But no problem. Must be a latex allergy, is Ted's diagnosis. Just stay out of the latex gloves we use for particularly nasty work; he'll give me another kind to wear.

I should, if I were going to stay in character, find an emergency room after work and try to cop a little charitable care. But it's too much. The itching gets so bad at night that I have mini-tantrums, waving my arms and stamping my feet to keep from scratching or bawling. So I fall back on the support networks of my real-life social class, call the dermatologist I know in Key West, and bludgeon him into prescribing something sight unseen. The whole episode—including anti-itch cream, prednisone, prednisone cream, and Benadryl to get through the nights—eats up $30. It's still unseasonably hot, and I often get to look out on someone's azure pool while I vacuum or scrub, frantic with suppressed itching. Even the rash-free are affected by the juxtaposition of terrible heat and cool, inaccessible water. In the car on one of the hottest days, after cleaning a place with pool, pool house, and gazebo, Rosalie and Maddy and I obsess about immersion in all imaginable forms—salt water versus fresh, lakes versus pools, surf versus smooth, glasslike surfaces. We can't even wash our hands in the houses, at least not after the sinks have been dried and buffed, and when I do manage to get a wash in before the sinks are off-limits, there's always some filthy last-minute job like squeezing out the rags used on floors once we get out of a house. Maybe I picked up some bug at a house or maybe it's the disinfectant I squirt on my hands, straight from the bottle, in an attempt at cleanliness. Three days into the rash, I make another trip to Old Orchard Beach and wade into the water with my clothes on (I didn't think to bring a bathing suit from Key West to Maine), trying to pretend that it's an accident when a wave washes over me and that I'm not just some pathetic street person using the beach as a bathtub.

There's something else working against my mood of muscular elation. I had been gloating internally about my ability to keep up with, and sometimes outwork, women twenty or thirty years younger than myself, but it turns out this comparative advantage says less about me than it does about them. Ours is a physical bond, to the extent that we bond at all. One person's infirmity can be a teammate's extra burden; there's a constant traffic in herbal and over-the-counter solutions to pain. If I don't know how my coworkers survive on their wages or what they make of our hellish condition, I do know about their back pains and cramps and arthritic attacks. Lori and Pauline are excused from vacuuming on account of their backs, which means you dread being assigned to a team with them. Helen has a bum foot, which Ted, in explaining her absence one day, blames on the cheap, ill-fitting shoes that, he implies, she perversely chooses to wear. Marge's arthritis makes scrubbing a torture; another woman has to see a physical therapist for her rotator cuff. When Rosalie tells me that she got her shoulder problem picking blueberries as a "kid"—she still is one in my eyes, of course—I flash on a scene from my own childhood, of wandering through fields on an intense July day, grabbing berries by the handful as I go. But when Rosalie was a kid she worked in the blueberry fields of northern Maine, and the damage to her shoulder is an occupational injury.

So ours is a world of pain—managed by Excedrin and Advil, compensated for with cigarettes and, in one or two cases and then only on weekends, with booze. Do the owners have any idea of the misery that goes into rendering their homes motel-perfect? Would they be bothered if they did know, or would they take a sadistic pride in what they have purchased—boasting to dinner guests, for example, that their floors are cleaned only with the purest of fresh human tears? In one of my few exchanges with an owner, a pert muscular woman whose desk reveals that she works part-time as a personal trainer, I am vacuuming and she notices the sweat. "That's a real workout, isn't it?" she observes, not unkindly, and actually offers me a glass of water, the only such offer I ever encounter. Flouting the rule against the ingestion of anything while inside a house, I take it, leaving an inch undrunk to avoid the awkwardness of a possible refill offer. "I tell all my clients," the trainer informs me, "'If you want to be fit, just fire your cleaning lady and do it yourself.'" "Ho ho," is all I say, since we're not just chatting in the gym together and I can't explain that this form of exercise is totally asymmetrical, brutally repetitive, and as likely to destroy the musculoskeletal structure as to strengthen it.

Self-restraint becomes more of a challenge when the owner of a million-dollar condo (that's my guess anyway, because it has three floors and a wide-angle view of the fabled rockbound coast) who is (according to a framed photograph on the wall) an acquaintance of the real Barbara Bush takes me into the master bathroom to explain the difficulties she's been having with the shower stall. Seems its marble walls have been "bleeding" onto the brass fixtures, and can I scrub the grouting extra hard? That's not your marble bleeding, I want to tell her, it's the worldwide working class—the people who quarried the marble, wove your Persian rugs until they went blind, harvested the apples in your lovely fall-themed dining room centerpiece, smelted the steel for the nails, drove the trucks, put up this building, and now bend and squat and sweat to clean it.

Not that I, even in my more histrionic moments, imagine that I am a member of that oppressed working class. My very ability to work tirelessly hour after hour is a product of decades of better-than-average medical care, a high-protein diet, and workouts in gyms that charge $400 or $500 a year. If I am now a productive fake member of the working class, it's because I haven't been working, in any hard physical sense, long enough to have ruined my body. But I will say this for myself: I have never employed a cleaning person or service (except, on two occasions, to prepare my house for a short-term tenant) even though various partners and husbands have badgered me over the years to do so. When I could have used one, when the kids were little, I couldn't afford it; and later, when I could afford it, I still found the idea repugnant. Partly this comes from having a mother who believed that a self-cleaned house was the hallmark of womanly virtue. Partly it's because my own normal work is sedentary, so that the housework I do—in dabs of fifteen minutes here and thirty minutes there—functions as a break. But mostly I rejected the idea, even after all my upper-middle-class friends had, guiltily and as covertly as possible, hired help for themselves, because this is just not the kind of relationship I want to have with another human being.[11]

[11] In 1999, somewhere between 14 and 18 percent of households employed an outsider to do the cleaning and the numbers are rising dramatically. Mediamark Research reports a 53 percent increase, between 1995 and 1999, in the number of households using a hired cleaner or service once a month or more, and Maritz Marketing finds that 30 percent of the people who hired help in 1999 had done so for the first time that year.

Managers of the new corporate cleaning services, such as the one I worked for, attribute their success not only to the influx of women into the workforce but to the tensions over housework that arose in its wake. When the trend toward hiring out was just beginning to take off, in 1988, the owner of a Merry Maids franchise in Arlington, Massachusetts, told the *Christian Science Monitor,* "I kid some women. I say, 'We even save marriages. In this new eighties period you expect more from the male partner, but very often you don't get the cooperation you would like to have. The alternative is to pay somebody to come in'" ("Ambushed by Dust Bunnies," *Christian Science Monitor,* April 4, 1988). Another Merry Maids franchise owner has learned to capitalize more directly on housework-related spats; he closes 30–35 percent of his sales by making follow-up calls Saturdays between 9:00 and 11:00 A.M.—which is "prime time for arguing over the fact that the house is a mess" ("Homes Harbor Dirty Secrets," *Chicago Tribune,* May 5, 1994).

Let's talk about shit, for example. It happens, as the bumper sticker says, and it happens to a cleaning person every day. The first time I encountered a shit-stained toilet as a maid, I was shocked by the sense of unwanted intimacy. A few hours ago, some well-fed butt was straining away on this toilet seat, and now here I am wiping up after it. For those who have never cleaned a really dirty toilet, I should explain that there are three kinds of shit stains. There are remnants of landslides running down the inside of toilet bowls. There are the splash-back remains on the underside of toilet seats. And, perhaps most repulsively, there's sometimes a crust of brown on the rim of a toilet seat, where a turd happened to collide on its dive to the water. You don't want to know this? Well, it's not something I would have chosen to dwell on myself, but the different kinds of stains require different cleaning approaches. One prefers those that are interior to the toilet bowl, since they can be attacked by brush, which is a kind of action-at-a-distance weapon. And one dreads the crusts on the seats, especially when they require the intervention of a Dobie as well as a rag.

Or we might talk about that other great nemesis of the bathroom cleaner—pubic hair. I don't know what it is about the American upper class, but they seem to be shedding their pubic hair at an alarming rate. You find it in quantity in shower stalls, bathtubs, Jacuzzis, drains, and even, unaccountably, in sinks. Once I spent fifteen minutes crouching in a huge four-person Jacuzzi, maddened by the effort of finding the dark little coils camouflaged against the eggplant-colored ceramic background but fascinated by the image of the pubes of the economic elite, which must by this time be completely bald.

There are worse things that owners can do, of course, than shit or shed. They can spy on us, for example. When I ask a teammate why the rule against cursing in houses, she says that owners have been known to leave tape recorders going while we work. Video cameras are another part of the lore, positioned near valuables to catch a cleaner in an act of theft. Whether any of this is true or not, Ted encourages us to imagine that we are under surveillance at all times in each house.[12] Other owners set traps for us. In one house, I am reprimanded by the team leader for failing to vacuum far enough under the Persian rugs scattered around on the hardwood floors, because this owner likes to leave little mounds of dirt there just so she can see if they're still there when we're done. More commonly, owners will arrange to be home when we come so they can check up on us while we work. I am vacuuming the home of a retired couple and happen to look into a room I've completed, where I see the female owner's enormous purple-encased butt staring up at me from the floor. I wouldn't have thought she was agile enough, but she's climbed under a desk to search out particles of overlooked dust.

I would say more about the houses themselves, but I lack the vocabulary for all the forms of wall finishings, flooring materials, light fixtures, fireplace equipment, porches, and statuary we encounter. On the subject of interior decorating, my general feeling has long been that it's too bad we're fur-less and have to live indoors. The various consequences of this infirmity—as manifested in architecture, furniture, etc.—have never managed to engage my attention. Far more useful to me,

---

[12] At the time, I dismissed this as a scare story, but I have since come across ads for concealable video cameras, like the Tech-7 "incredible coin-sized camera" designed to "get a visual record of your babysitter's actions" and "watch employees to prevent theft."

for understanding the tics, pretensions, and insecurities of the
owner class, are books and other print-related artifacts. I learn
that one of our owners is a Scientologist; another proudly
claims descent from one of the same Scottish clans my own
ancestors belonged to. Still another has framed a certificate
announcing that she is listed in the *Who's Who of American
Women.* As for books, at the low end of the literacy spectrum,
which is where most of our clients dwell, I find Grisham and
Limbaugh; at the high end, there's a lot of Amy Tan and I once
even spotted an Ondaatje. Mostly, though, books are for show,
and real life—judging from the quantity of food stains and
tossed items of clothing—goes on in the room that houses the
large-screen TV. The only books that seriously offend me are
the antique ones, no doubt purchased in bulk, that are sometimes deployed on end tables for purposes of quaintness and
"authenticity"—as if the owners actually spent their spare
moments reading a 1920 title like *Bobsledding in Vermont: One
Boy's Adventure.* But time pressures inevitably curtail my literary investigations. The real issue for a maid is the *number* of
books per shelf: if that number is greater than twelve, we can
treat them as a single mass and dust around them; otherwise
each one must be removed and dusted separately.

Not all of our owners are rich. Maybe a quarter to a third of
the houses look to be merely middle-class and some of these—
probably because they lack interim help to do the light cleaning between our visits every week or two—are seriously dirty.
But class is a relative thing. Once, after polishing up two houses
in which the number of occupants clearly exceeded the number of bathrooms—an unmistakable sign of financial impair-
ment, along with the presence of teddy bears in decorative
roles—I asked Holly, my team leader of the day, whether the

next house on our list was "wealthy." Her answer: "If we're cleaning their house, they're wealthy."

IT IS UNDENIABLY FALL WHEN I FIND MYSELF BEING ASSIGNED, DAY after day, to Holly's team. There's fog in the morning now and the farm stands are pushing pumpkins. On the radio in our company car the classic rock station notes the season by playing "Maggie May" several times a day—*It's late September and I really should be BACK at school.* Other people are going out to their offices or classrooms; we stay behind, Cinderella-like, in their usually deserted homes. On the pop station, it's Pearl Jam's hypnotic "Last Kiss," so beautifully sad, it makes bereavement seem like an enviable condition. Not that we ever comment on what the radio brings us or on any other part of the world outside The Maids and its string of client houses. In this, the most dutiful and serious of all the teams I have been on, the conversation, at least in the morning, is all about the houses that lie ahead. *Murphy—isn't that the one that took four hours the first time? Yeah, but it's OK once you get past the master bath, which you've gotta use mold killer on . . .* And so on. Or we pass around our routing sheet and study the day's owners' "Hot Buttons," as sketched in by Tammy. Typical "Hot Buttons" are baseboards, windowsills, and ceiling fans—never, of course, poverty, racism, or global warming.

But the relevant point about Holly is that she is visibly unwell—possibly whiter, on a daily basis, than anyone else in the state. We're not just talking Caucasian here; think bridal gowns, tuberculosis, and death. All I know about her is that she is twenty-three, has been married for almost a year, and manages to feed her husband, herself, and an elderly relative on $30–$50 a week, which is only a little more than what I spend on food for myself. I'd be surprised if she weighs more than ninety-two pounds before breakfast, assuming breakfast is even on her agenda. During an eight-to-nine-hour shift, I never see her eat more than one of those tiny cracker sandwiches with peanut butter filling, and you would think she had no use for food at all if it weren't for the fact that every afternoon at about 2:30 she starts up a food-fantasy conversation in the car. "What did you have for dinner last night, Marge?" she'll ask, Marge being our oldest and most affluent team member, who—thanks to a working commercial fisherman husband—sometimes brings reports from such fine-dining spots as T.G.I. Friday's. Or we'll drive by a Dairy Queen and Holly will say, "They have great foursquares"—the local name for a sundae—"there, you know. With four kinds of sauce. You get chocolate, strawberry, butterscotch, and marshmallow and any kind of ice cream you want. I had one once and let it get a little melted and, oh my *God*," etc.

Today, though, even Marge, who normally chatters on obliviously about the events in her life ("It was the *biggest* spider" or "So she just puts a little mustard right in with the baked beans . . ."), notices how shaky Holly looks. "Is it just indigestion or is there nausea?" she asks. When Holly admits to nausea, Marge wants to know if she's pregnant. No answer. Marge asks again, and again no answer. "I'm *talking* to you, Holly, *answer* me." It's a tense moment, with Marge prying and Holly just as rudely stonewalling, but Holly, as team leader, prevails.

There are only the three of us—Denise is out with a migraine—and at the first house I suggest that Marge and I do all the vacuuming for the day. Marge doesn't chime in on my offer, but it doesn't matter since Holly says no way. I resolve to race through dusting so I can take over as much as possible from Holly. When I finish, I rush to the kitchen, only to find a scene so melodramatic that for a second I think I have walked out of *Dusting,* the videotape, and into an entirely different movie. Holly is in a distinctly un-team-leader-like position, standing slumped over a counter with her head on her arms. "I shouldn't be here today," she says, looking up wanly. "I had a big fight with my husband. I didn't want to go to work this morning but he said I had to." This confidence is so completely out of character that I'm speechless. She goes on. The problem is probably that she's pregnant. It's been seven weeks and the nausea is out of control, which is why she can't eat anything and gets so weak, but she wants it to be a secret until she can tell Ted herself.

Very tentatively and mindful of the deep reserve of rural Mainers, as explained to me by a sociologist acquaintance, I touch her arm and tell her she shouldn't be doing this. Even if she were feeling OK she probably shouldn't be around the chemicals we use. She should go home. But all I can talk her into is taking the Pure Protein sports bar I always carry in my bag in case my sandwich lets me down. At first she refuses it. Then, when I repeat the offer, she says, "Really?" and finally takes it, picking off little chunks with trembling fingertips and cramming them into her mouth. Also, would I mind doing the driving for the rest of the day because she doesn't trust herself on account of the dizziness?

For the first time in my life as a maid I have a purpose more compelling than trying to meet the aesthetic standards of the New England bourgeoisie. I will do the work of two people, if necessary three. The next house belongs to a woman known to Holly and Marge as a "friggin' bitch," who turns out to be Martha Stewart or at least a very dedicated acolyte thereof.

Everything about it enrages me, and some of it would be irritating even if I were just dropping by for cocktails and not toiling alongside this pale, undernourished child: the brass plaque on the door announcing the date of construction (mid-eighteenth century), the wet bar with its ostentatious alignment of single-malt Scotches, the four-poster king-sized bed with canopy, the Jacuzzi so big you have to climb stairs to get into it and probably safe for diving when filled. I whiz through the bathrooms and even manage to complete the kitchen while the others are still on their initial tasks. Then Marge shows up in the kitchen and points out the row of copper pots and pans hanging from a rack near the ceiling. According to our instructions, she informs me, every one of them has to be taken down and polished with the owner's special polish.

OK. The only way to get to them is to climb up on the kitchen counter, kneel there, and reach up for them from that position. These are not pots for cooking, I should point out, just decorative pots deployed to catch stray beams of sunlight or reflect the owners' no doubt expensively buffed and peeled faces. The final pot is unexpectedly heavy—they are arranged in size order—and as I grasp it from my crouching position on the countertop, it slips from my hand and comes crashing down into a fishbowl cunningly furnished with marbles. Fish fly, marbles skitter all over the floor, and water—which in our work is regarded as a dangerous contaminant—soaks everything, including a stack of cookbooks containing *Cucina Simpatica,* a number of works set in Provence, and, yes, Martha Stewart herself. No one gets mad at me, not even Ted, back in the office, who is bonded for this sort of thing. My punishment is seeing Holly's face, when she rushes into the kitchen to see what the crash was, completely polarized with fear.

After the accident, Holly decides we can take a convenience store break. I buy myself a pack of cigarettes and sit out in the rain to puff (I haven't inhaled for years but it helps anyway) while the others drink their Cokes in the car. Have to get over this savior complex, I instruct myself, no one wants to be rescued by a klutz. Even my motives seem murky at the moment. Yes, I want to help Holly and everyone else in need, on a worldwide basis if possible. I am a "good person," as my demented charges at the nursing home agree, but maybe I'm also just sick of my suddenly acquired insignificance. Maybe I want to "be somebody," as Jesse Jackson likes to say, somebody generous, competent, brave, and perhaps, above all, noticeable.

Maids, as an occupational group, are not visible, and when we are seen we are often sorry for it.[13] On the way to the Martha Stewart–ish place, when Holly and Marge were complaining about her haughtiness in a past encounter, I had ventured to ask why so many of the owners seem hostile or contemptuous

---

[13] This invisibility persists at the macroscopic level. The Census Bureau reports that there were 550,000 domestic workers in 1998, up 10 percent since 1996, but this may be a considerable underestimate, since so much of the servant economy is still underground, or at least very low to the ground, where few data collectors ever venture. In 1993, for example, the year when Zoë Baird lost her chance to be attorney general for paying her undocumented nanny off the books, it was estimated that fewer than 10 percent of those Americans who paid a housecleaner more than $1,000 a year reported these payments to the IRS. Sociologist Mary Romero offers an example of how severe the undercounting can be: the 1980 census found only 1,063 "private household workers" in El Paso, although at the same time that city's Department of Planning, Research, and Development estimated their numbers at 13,400 and local bus drivers estimated that half of the 28,300 bus trips taken daily were taken by maids going to and returning from work (*Maid in the U.S.A.,* p. 92). The honesty of employers has increased since the Baird scandal, but most experts believe that household workers remain largely uncounted and invisible to the larger economy.

toward us. "They think we're stupid," was Holly's answer. "They think we have nothing better to do with our time." Marge too looked suddenly sober. "We're nothing to these people," she said. "We're just maids." Nor are we much of anything to anyone else. Even convenience store clerks, who are $6-an-hour gals themselves, seem to look down on us. In Key West, my waitress's polo shirt was always a conversation starter: "You at Jerry's?" a clerk might ask. "I used to work at the waffle place just up the boulevard from there." But a maid's uniform has the opposite effect. At one place where we stopped for refreshments, an actual diner with a counter, I tried to order iced tea to take out, but the waitress just kept standing there chatting with a coworker, ignoring my "Excuse me's." Then there's the supermarket. I used to stop on my way home from work, but I couldn't take the stares, which are easily translatable into: What are *you* doing here? And, No wonder she's poor, she's got a beer in her shopping cart! True, I don't look so good by the end of the day and probably smell like eau de toilet and sweat, but it's the brilliant green-and-yellow uniform that gives me away, like prison clothes on a fugitive. Maybe, it occurs to me, I'm getting a tiny glimpse of what it would be like to be black.

And look at me now, sitting on a curb at a gas station, puffing into the endless slow rain, so sweat-soaked already that it doesn't matter. Things don't get any more squalid than this, is my thought. But they can—they can!—and they do. At the next house, I am getting my toilet brush out of its Ziploc bag when the liquid that's been accumulating in the bag all day spills on my foot—100 percent pure toilet juice leaking through the laces and onto my sock. In ordinary life, if someone were to, say, piss on your foot, you'd probably strip off the shoe and the sock and throw them away. But these are the only shoes I have. There's nothing to do but try to ignore the nasty stuff soaking my foot and, as Ted exhorts us, work through it.

MESSAGE TO ME FROM MY FORMER SELF: SLOW DOWN AND, ABOVE all, detach. If you can't stand being around suffering people, then you have no business in the low-wage work world, as a journalist or anything else. Besides, I have problems of my own to attend to, most urgently money. My initial calculations suggested that I would do very well with my two jobs—in the long run, that is, and if nothing untoward occurred. But there was no check for me my first Friday at The Maids since, I am informed, a new employee's first paycheck is withheld until she eventually leaves or quits, apparently to keep her from rushing off on a spending spree and failing to show up for the second week. In addition to rash-related expenses, I am unpleasantly surprised to discover that the rent for my first week at the Blue Haven is $200, not $120, because the tourist season was not yet deemed completely over. Plus, since my apartment, though rented as "furnished," contained almost no kitchen items when I moved in, I was forced to acquire my own inventory of spatula, can opener, "utility knife," broom, etc., at Wal-Mart. I will be fine once the paychecks start rolling in from both places of work, but now, late in my second week of employment, I foresee a lean weekend, even taking into account free lunches at the Woodcrest.

Is there help for the hardworking poor? Yes, but it takes a determined and not too terribly poor person to find it. On a Thursday after work, I drive to the Mobil station across the street from The Maids and call the Prebles Street Resource Center, which is listed in the phone book as a source of free meals and all-around help. I get a recorded message saying that

Prebles Street closes at 3:00 P.M.—so much for the working poor!—but to try 774-HELP after that. There I wait on hold for four minutes before someone picks up. I tell him I am new to the area and employed but need some immediate food aid or cash assistance. Why do I need money if I'm employed, he wants to know—didn't I bring any money with me? It got used up on housing, I tell him, which was more expensive than I'd expected. Well, why didn't I check out the rents before I moved here, then? I had thought of telling him about the rash too, as a mitigating circumstance, but decide that our relationship is not at a point where I want to be discussing my body. Finally, he yields and gives me another number. A sequence of four more calls ensues before I reach a helpful human, Gloria, who says I should go to the food pantry in Biddeford tomorrow between nine and five. What is this assumption that the hungry are free all day to drive around visiting "community action centers" and charitable agencies? So Gloria sends me to Karen at another number, another voluntary agency, where I am told I am in the wrong county. Very slowly, and trying to adopt the same businesslike tone I would use if I were calling to inquire about a credit card statement, I run through my time and geography constraints once again, underscoring that I work seven days a week, at least eight hours a day, and that I happen to be in her geographical jurisdiction at the moment. Bingo! Karen relents. I can't have cash, but she'll make a call and I can pick up a food voucher at a South Portland Shop-n-Save. What would I like for dinner?

The question seems frivolous or mocking. What do I want for dinner? How about polenta-crusted salmon filet with pesto sauce and a nice glass of J. Lohr Chardonnay? But Karen is serious. I can't have cash, which, God forbid, I would blow at a liquor store, but neither can I have any old food item that might appeal. My dinner choices, she explains, are limited to any two of the following: one-box spaghetti noodles, one jar spaghetti sauce, one can of vegetables, one can of baked beans, one pound of hamburger, a box of Hamburger Helper, or a box of Tuna Helper. No fresh fruit or vegetables, no chicken or cheese, and, oddly, no tuna to help out with. For breakfast I can have cereal and milk or juice. Good enough. I drive to the Shop-n-Save, pick up my voucher (which again lists my meager options) at Customer Service, and commence to shop and certainly save. I get a quart of milk, a box of cereal, a pound of chopped meat, and a can of kidney beans, figuring that the latter two will make a sort of chili or at least refried beans con carne, and fortunately the checkout woman doesn't challenge my substitution of kidney beans for baked ones. I attempt to thank her, but she is looking the other way at nothing in particular. Bottom line: $7.02 worth of food acquired in seventy minutes of calling and driving, minus $2.80 for the phone calls—which ends up being equivalent to a wage of $3.63 an hour.

Then there are weekends at the Woodcrest. I have been trying to interpret them as genuine weekends, as if, after spending the weekdays on futile and largely cosmetic labor, I had decided to volunteer to do something useful for a change. "It must be so depressing," my sister and, of course, fellow Alzheimer's orphan writes to me, but not at all. Once you join the residents in forgetting about the functioning humans they once were, you can think of them as a band of wizened toddlers at a tea party. Then too, compared with the women at The Maids, my Woodcrest coworkers are an enthusiastic and outgoing bunch, though the faces tend to change from one weekend to the next. By carving out a little space from Pete—partly because I don't want to fall into the habit of social smoking—I get to at least the "Hi there" level with a dozen or so cooks, nurses, CNAs, and other dietary aides. Mostly, I relish the autonomy and minute-by-minute freedom of motion. Weekends are notoriously supervisor-free, and Linda, who is hardly a dictator anyway, seldom reappears after day one. I can start setting tables or sweeping from any part of the room I feel like; none of that left-to-right, top-to-bottom stuff here. I can decide whether we're going to need more ice cream for the lunch service and whether it will be chocolate ripple or strawberry. If a resident is rejecting the chicken tenders or meat balls we have on the menu, I can propose an alternative on my own: What if I just make you up a nice grilled cheese sandwich and some hot tomato soup? I launder the napkins and tablecloths entirely at my own discretion.

But there can be too much freedom and certainly far too much motion. On the Saturday after the fishbowl incident, I arrive at seven to find that my fellow dietary aide for the day has gone AWOL and that I will be the sole dietary worker on the locked Alzheimer's ward. Furthermore, neither Pete nor any of the other cooks in the main kitchen seems to be available to perform their usual breakfast function of loading up plates in the ward's little kitchen while I do the serving. The "furthermores" multiply: it turns out the upstairs dishwasher, the one convenient to the Alzheimer's ward, is broken, meaning that the dishware has to be prewashed upstairs, then hauled downstairs by cart to the working dishwasher just off the main kitchen. As a final malicious touch, the set of keys I need to get into the upstairs kitchen and, of course, out of the locked ward are missing, so that I have to track down a nurse every time I need a door opened. I have very little memory of this day, and my journal notes for it have the gasping, panicky tone of e-mails from an Everest climber who has just used up her last oxygen canister: "Scrape and rinse plates and load cart for first trip downstairs to working dishwasher. Put away unused food items (syrup, milk, etc.). Bring back first load of clean dishes and put them away in upstairs pantry. Collect tablecloths, place mats, and napkins and throw them in washer. Sweep under chairs. Vacuum around chairs." I get through it, thanks to the nurse's aides who pitch in with serving, and thanks also to a lesson I learned while waitressing at Jerry's: Don't stop, don't think, don't even pause for an instant, because if you do, you'll be aware of the weariness taking over your legs, and then it will win.

After work I decide to visit the state park where Pete has been threatening to take me, to appropriate a bit of this brilliant fall day for myself. Children are climbing around on the huge black rocks that abut the ocean and normally I would do so too, but the legs that served me so well for hours are rubbery now, so I just sit on a rock and stare. What is this business of letting someone in off the street to run a nursing home, or at least a vital chunk of a nursing home, for a day?[14] True, this is

[14] A report issued by the U.S. Department of Health and Human Services in July 2000 found most nursing homes dangerously understaffed, especially profit-making nursing homes, such as the one where I worked. Among the consequences of understaffing, according to the report, are increases in preventable problems like severe bedsores, malnutrition, dehydration, congestive heart failure, and infections. While I never saw a patient neglected or mistreated in the dining area where I worked at the Woodcrest, it would have been easy for an aide to make a life-threatening mistake, such as serving sugar-containing foods to a diabetic. I consider myself—and my patients—extremely fortunate that I did not inadvertently harm someone on this day when I fed the Alzheimer's ward by myself.

the one job where my references were actually checked, but what if I were one of those angel-of-death type health workers, who decided to free my charges from their foggy half-lives? More to the point, I am wondering what the two-job way of life would do to a person after a few months with zero days off. In my writing life I normally work seven days a week, but writing is ego food, totally self-supervised and intermittently productive of praise. Here, no one will notice my heroism on that Saturday's shift. (I will later make a point of telling Linda about it and receive only a distracted nod.) If you hump away at menial jobs 360-plus days a year, does some kind of repetitive injury of the spirit set in?

I don't know and I don't intend to find out, but I can guess that one of the symptoms is a bad case of tunnel vision. Work fills the landscape; coworkers swell to the size of family members or serious foes. Slights loom large, and a reprimand can reverberate into the night. If I make some vacuuming error, which I do often enough, I can expect to spend part of my evening reviewing it and rebutting the reprimand: "But the tape didn't *say* go halfway under the throw rugs," and so on, not that I remember the tape. The Sunday night after my solo performance at the Woodcrest, I wake up at three in the morning gripped by the theory that Pete had deliberately set me up. He *should* have been there with me loading plates, but he must have gotten pissed because I hadn't been showing up for cigarette dates and decided to try to derail me. As it turns out, the theory is groundless; on the next Saturday, Pete even brings me a homemade Egg McMuffin as a treat. But the fact that I could have used up precious sleep time imagining I'd been stabbed in the back is alarming enough. Whoa, girl, time to get a grip!

The goal for my third week at The Maids is to achieve a state of transcendent detachment. Anger is toxic, as the New Agers say, and there is no evidence anyway that my coworkers share my outrage on their behalf, at least not in any overt form. There are only two forms of rebellion I have seen any evidence of and neither of them challenges the vaulting social hierarchy above us. One is theft. I never observe anyone stealing, but the possibility is a persistent subtext of The Maids' discipline and lore. Our garish uniforms and bright green-and-yellow cars, for example, are probably designed to distinguish us from the average crew of burglars, and I suspect that the reason there are no back pockets in our slacks is to discourage us from filling them with jewelry and coins. Some owners leave out rolls of coins or even stacks of loose bills, perhaps with a video camera trained on them to catch some light-fingered or especially hungry maid in the act. At one morning meeting, Ted gravely informs us that there has just been "an incident" and that the perpetrator is no longer with us. This kind of thing hardly ever happens, he says, because the Accutrac test is almost 100 percent reliable in weeding out dishonest people (with the exception of myself, of course).

The other form of rebellion consists of public violations of The Maids' code of decorum. A couple of my coworkers— team leaders, in fact—delight in putting the pedal to the metal and terrorizing the elegant neighborhoods we serve. I wouldn't be surprised if complaints have gotten back to Ted about one particular joyride where the driver (who will not even be identified by her made-up name, lest some other characteristic give her away) decided to go screeching around a neighborhood containing several of our houses, blaring out a rap tape consisting largely of the words "FUCK YOU, ASSHOLE" and kinky permutations thereof, while an owner type pushing a stroller cringed on the sidewalk. We laughed ourselves silly in the backseat, clutching our armrests and trying not to get sick. But this kind of rebellion threatens only the rare pedestrian member of the owning class. For the most part, my coworkers seem content to occupy their little niche on the sheer cliff face of class inequality. After all, if there weren't people who have far too much money and floor space and stuff, there could hardly be maids.

So bit by bit, while scrubbing and Windexing and buffing, I cobble together a philosophy of glorious nonattachment. I draw on the Jesus who was barred from the tent revival, the one who said that the last shall be first and that, if someone asks for your cloak, give him your robe as well. I throw in a dab of secondhand Buddhism remembered from a friend's account of a monastery in northern California where rich people pay to spend their weekends meditating and doing various menial chores, housework included. When I first heard of this monastery I laughed out loud, but now the image of dot-com moguls scrubbing for the good of their souls presents itself as a psychic flotation device. Then there is the fact, offered to me by my son in a phone conversation, that Simone Weil once worked in a factory for some metaphysical purpose I could not entirely comprehend, so I add a little of that to the blend. In the beautiful fantasy that results, I am not working for a maid service; rather, I have joined a mystic order dedicated to performing the most despised of tasks, cheerfully and virtually for free—grateful, in fact, for this chance to earn grace through submission and toil. Holly can bleed to death in my presence if she likes, and I will just consider her to be specially favored by an inscrutable God, more or less as Jesus was. I decide not even to complain about having my first paycheck withheld or the ways we're shortchanged every day. We're told to get to work at 7:30, but the meter doesn't start running until about 8:00, when we take off in the cars, and there's no pay for the half hour or so we spend in the office at the end of the day, sorting out the dirty rags before they're washed and refilling our cleaning fluid bottles. But why complain about not being paid, when those people at the Buddhist monastery pay with their own money to do the same kind of work?

The exalted mood lasts for about a day, and there is backsliding even within that—for example, when, in a huge, gorgeous country house with hand-painted walls, I encounter a shelf full of arrogant and, under the circumstances, personally insulting neoconservative encomiums to the status quo and consider using germ warfare against the owners, the weapons for which are within my apron pockets. All I would have to do is take one of the *E. coli*–rich rags that's been used on the toilets and use it to "clean" the kitchen counters—a plan that entertains me for an hour or more. But it is, weirdly enough, the home of an actual Buddhist that shatters the sanctified mood. We encounter many signs of "spirituality" among the owners—books like *Ten Things I Learned about Life in My Garden* and inspirational wall hangings urging centeredness. But this is the home of a genuine Buddhist—a Caucasian convert, of course—complete with Zen paperbacks and a three-foot-high statue of the Buddha in the living room, with a note affixed to his serene and creaseless forehead warning that we are not to touch him, not even to dust.

As we leave, in our usual rush to get the buckets to the car, Holly trips in a hole in the ground and falls down and screams. I whirl around and she's crying, her face gone from dead-white to crimson. "Something snapped," she sobs, "I heard it snap." I help her up, ordering Marge, who's been standing there with her mouth hanging open, to take her other arm. "We've got to get you to an emergency room," I say, "get it X-rayed right away." But no, all she'll consent to is calling Ted from the next house, although Denise is going to have to do the driving. I keep trying in the car, blabbing about fractures and sprains as if I actually knew something, but Holly just keeps crying and talking about how she's already missed so many days of work in the last few weeks, and the others don't seem to be listening to either of us.

When we get to the house, Holly lets me look at the ankle, and while I'm bent over it—not that there's anything to see— she whispers that the pain is really wicked now. "You can't work," I say. "You hear me, Holly? You *can't* work on this ankle." Still, all she'll agree to do is call Ted from the phone in the kitchen, and I stand there listening to her apologize weepily to him, throwing in a bit about how Barbara is making a fuss, and I feel the beautiful Zen detachment drain out of me with the sweat on my face. I reach out and insist that she give me the phone, and the first words I hear, almost before I can say, "Listen," are "Now let's just calm down, Barbara," although he's old enough to know that "calm down" generally functions as an incitement to rage.

I blow. I can't remember the exact words, but I tell him he can't keep putting money above his employees' health and I don't want to hear about "working through it," because this girl is in really bad shape. But he just goes on about "calm down," and meanwhile Holly is hopping around the bathroom, wiping up pubic hairs.

I hang up on him and follow Holly into the bathroom to take my stand. Should I say, "Look, I'm actually a highly educated person, a Ph.D., in fact, and I can't just stand by and . . ."? But it would sound crazy and what would Holly care? For all I know, her husband beats her for missing work. So I do the only other thing I can think of. I say, "I'm not working if you don't get help. Or at least sit down with your foot up while we do your work." I look to Denise, who is peering into the bathroom after us, for support. "This is a work stoppage. Ever hear of that? This is a strike." Denise just goes back to work, crinkling her face up in embarrassment or maybe disgust.

"I'm just doing bathrooms," Holly says, to appease me.

"What, on one foot?"

"I come from a stubborn family."

"Well, so the hell do I."

But Holly's ancestors win out over mine. The team leader in her prevails over the mother in me. If I walk out, where am I going to walk to, anyway? Outside, horses graze in a meadow, migrating birds dip and rise in perfect formation. I don't have any idea where I am—north of Portland, west? I could call a cab but I don't have enough cash for the trip home or any cash waiting for me there. I could get on one of those horses, if I knew how to ride a horse, and gallop from meadow to meadow, through backyards and highways, all the way out to the sea. But the only thing I'd accomplish by leaving, assuming there was a way to leave, would be to increase the workload on the other three, Holly included, because she's going to keep going until you pry the last cleaning rag from her cold, dead hands, she's made that clear enough.

So there's nothing to do but swallow it. Shaking with anger (at Ted), betrayal (in the cases of Marge and Denise), and most of all at my own total, abject helplessness, I shoulder the vacuum and strap myself in. It's not easy focusing on throw rugs when all I can see is this grass fire raging in the back of my eyes, white-hot and devouring house after house as it burns. I screw up big-time, as Denise points out with what is now obvious malice, and have to do the downstairs all over again. In the car there is silence for a little while and nobody except Marge, who as usual has moved right along, will look at me. Then Holly starts up one of those pornographic late-afternoon food conversations she enjoys so much. "What are you making for dinner tonight, Marge? . . . Oh yeah, with tomato sauce?"

I sit in the car on the long ride back trying to keep rage alive by rehearsing what I'll say when Ted fires me for insubordination. "Look," I'll say, "I can put up with shit and snot and every other gross substance I encounter in this line of work. The only thing I'm squeamish about is human pain. I'm sorry, I tried to ignore it, but it undermines my efficiency when I have to work alongside people who are crying, fainting, starving, or otherwise visibly suffering, so yes, you better find someone tougher than me." Or some similar stiff little speech. When we're within a couple of blocks of the office, Marge turns to me with what looks like compassion. I know Marge doesn't come out looking too good in this story, but we've had some long, intimate talks about hormones and antidepressants and other middle-aged things. There was a day, too, when we teased each other for sweating so much, then, when the house was finished, ran out together in the rain, held our heads back and our arms out, laughing like pagans, and I loved her for that. Now she says, "You look tired, Barbara." The word is *defeated,* but I just say—loud enough to be heard by Holly and Denise in the front too—"I'm bracing for a confrontation with Ted."

"He's not going to fire you," Marge says brightly. "Don't worry about that."

"Oh, I'm not worried about it. There're millions of jobs out there. Look at the want ads." Denise turns partway around to regard me blankly from the side of her face. Don't they look at the want ads? Don't they realize that the sheer abundance of them means they've got Ted by the short hairs and could ask for almost anything—like, say, $7.50 an hour, reckoned from the moment they show up in the morning to the moment they finish processing rags at the end of the day?

"But we need you," Marge says. And then, as if that was too affectionate sounding: "You can't just leave Ted in the lurch."

"What's all this worrying about Ted? He'll find someone else. He'll take anyone who can manage to show up sober at 7:30 in the morning. Sober and standing upright."

"No," Holly finally interjects. "That's not true. Not everyone can get this job. You have to pass the test."

The test? The Accutrac test? "The test," I practically yell, "is BULLSHIT! *Anyone* can pass that test!"

It's an inexcusable outburst. First, because it's insulting, especially to Holly and the brittle sense of professionalism that keeps her going through sickness and injury. For all I know the test was a challenge to her at the level of basic literacy. Everyone here can read, but Holly has sometimes asked me how to spell words like *carry* and *weighed* that she needs to report any "incidents" that occur. Second, of course, because it's against the rules to use "bad words" in a company car. Where's *my* professionalism, anyway, the journalistic detachment that was supposed to guide and sustain me every inch of the way?

But misdirected rage is not an easy thing to hold on to; the last sparks of it get snuffed out, as they deserve to be, in the icy waters of humiliation and defeat. Holly will hate me forever, I can tell, both because I defied her authority as team leader and because I've had a chance, more than once now, to see her all tearful and scared. Denise will hate me, of course, for making a scene that made her uncomfortable or maybe just for slowing down the work. Marge will forget all about it. But even now, months later, I'm damned if I know how I should have handled the situation. By keeping my mouth shut in the first place, when Holly took her fall? Or by sticking to my one-person strike until—who knows?—she eventually relented and let us drive her to the nearest ER or at least sat down? The only thing I know for sure is that this is as low as I can get in my life as a maid, and probably in most other lives as well.

TED DOESN'T FIRE ME. THE NEXT MORNING I RUN INTO HOLLY IN THE parking lot, limping badly and heading back to her car. "Would you believe it?" she says, addressing Marge, who shows up at exactly that moment. "Ted sent me home!"—as if this were some arbitrary injustice. There were things I would have said if Marge weren't there, like "I'm sorry" and "Please take care of yourself." But the moment passes and my vindication, if that's what this is, tastes sour. In the office Ted thanks me for my "concern" and says he's taken my advice about Holly and sent her home. But—there has to be a "but"—you know you can't help someone who doesn't want to be helped. I guess it's the mother in me, is my lame response. To which he says, testily, "Well, I'm a parent too, and that doesn't make me less of a person." *Very* calmly, I am proud to report, I tell him, "It's supposed to make you *more* of a person."

I don't get the last word with Ted, of course. A couple of days later, I am out with the still-limping Holly, who continues to treat me like some nonhuman and slightly unreliable cleaning product—a defective Janitor in a Drum—when she gets a call via beeper from Ted that I'm to be driven back to the office and sent out to another team that's facing a rough first-timer. Why me? I don't know, maybe he just wants to talk to me. First thing he says as we head out, just him and me in the car, is how great I'm doing—he gets just great reports—so he's giving me a raise to $6.75 an hour. I can't believe this: smashing fishbowls and threatening work stoppages is doing great? But he's moved on to how he's not a bad guy, I should know this, and he cares a lot about his girls. See, he's got some great gals, like Holly and Liza, but there's a certain number of malcontents and he just wishes they'd stop their complaining. I know what he's talking about, right? This must be my cue to name a few names, because this is how Ted operates, my coworkers claim—through snitches and by setting up one woman against another. He's told us, for example, that if someone is absent it's up to the rest of us to get on her case, because we're the ones who'll suffer if our teams are shorthanded. But I use the occasion to ask him the question that's been bothering me since Holly's fall: Will she be paid for the day when he sent her home, since she was, after all, injured on the job? "Oh yes, of course"—but his chuckle seems a little forced—"What do you think I am, an ogre?" Well, no, though I don't say this, the word I am thinking of is *pimp*.

Why does anyone put up with this when there are so many other jobs available? In fact, one woman does leave for what she insists is a better job—working the counter at a Dunkin' Donuts. But there are some practical reasons for sticking with

The Maids: changing jobs means a week and possibly more without a paycheck; plus there's the attraction of the so-called "mothers' hours," although in practice we often end up working till five. The other, less tangible factor is the lure of Ted's approval. This, perhaps as much as the money, is what keeps Holly going through nausea and pain, and even some of the livelier, bolder women seem inordinately sensitive to how he's feeling about them. Getting "reamed out" by Ted can ruin their whole day; a morsel of praise will be savored for weeks. I see the power of his approval most clearly on Pauline's last day. She is sixty-seven and has been on the job longer than anyone—two years—enough to rate her a mention in the newsletter published by corporate headquarters. Her back has long since given out but she's leaving now because she's scheduled for knee surgery in a couple of weeks, the result, she says, of too much floor scrubbing. Still, Ted makes no mention of her departure at the morning meeting of her last day, nor does he thank her privately or wish her well at the end of the day. I know this because I offer her a ride home that day when it appears that her usual one isn't going to show up. As we drive through the rainy streets of South Portland, she talks about the surgery and the weeks of recovery that will follow it, and then the need to go out and find another job, preferably one that doesn't involve so much bending and lifting and crouching. But mostly she talks about Ted and her feeling of hurt. "He's never liked me since I had to stop vacuuming because of my back," she says. "I've asked him why I get paid less than anyone"—anyone at her level of seniority is, I think, what she means—"and he says, 'Well, if you could just vacuum . . .'" There's no bitterness in her voice, just the mortal sadness of looking ahead, toward the end of one's life, at the gray streets and the rain.

The big question is why Ted's approval means so much. As far as I can figure, my coworkers' neediness—because that's what it is—stems from chronic deprivation. The home owners aren't going to thank us for a job well done, and God knows, people on the street aren't going to hail us as heroines of proletarian labor. No one will know that the counter on which he slices the evening's baguette only recently supported a fainting woman—and decide to reward her with a medal for bravery. No one is going to say, after I vacuum ten rooms and still have time to scrub a kitchen floor, "Goddamn, Barb, you're good!" Work is supposed to save you from being an "outcast," as Pete puts it, but what we do is an outcast's work, invisible and even disgusting. Janitors, cleaning ladies, ditchdiggers, changers of adult diapers—these are the untouchables of a supposedly caste-free and democratic society. Hence the undeserved charisma of a man like Ted. He may be greedy and offhandedly cruel, but at The Maids he is the only living representative of that better world where people go to college and wear civilian clothes to work and shop on the weekends for fun. If for some reason there's a shortage of houses to clean, he'll keep a team busy by sending them out to clean his own home, which, I am told, is "real nice."

Or maybe it's low-wage work in general that has the effect of making you feel like a pariah. When I watch TV over my dinner at night, I see a world in which almost everyone makes $15 an hour or more, and I'm not just thinking of the anchor folks. The sitcoms and dramas are about fashion designers or schoolteachers or lawyers, so it's easy for a fast-food worker or nurse's aide to conclude that she is an anomaly—the only one, or almost the only one, who hasn't been invited to the party. And in a sense she would be right: the poor have disappeared from the culture at large, from its political rhetoric and intellectual endeavors as well as from its daily entertainment. Even religion seems to have little to say about the plight of the poor, if that tent revival was a fair sample. The moneylenders have finally gotten Jesus out of the temple.

On my last afternoon, I try to explain who I am and why I've been working here to the women on my team for the day, a much more spirited group than Holly's usual crew. My announcement attracts so little attention that I have to repeat it: "Will you listen to me? I'm a writer and I'm going to write a *book* about this place." At last Lori leans around from the front seat and hushes the others with "Hey, this is interesting," and to me: "Are you like, *investigating?*"

Well, not just this place and not exactly "investigating," but Lori has latched on to that concept. She hoots with laughter. "This place could *use* some investigating!" Now everyone seems to get it—not who I am or what I do—but that whatever I'm up to, the joke is on Ted.

At least now that I'm "out" I get to ask the question I've wanted to ask all this time: How do they feel, not about Ted but about the owners, who have so much while others, like themselves, barely get by? This is the answer from Lori, who at twenty-four has a serious disk problem and an $8,000 credit card debt: "All I can think of is like, wow, I'd like to have this stuff someday. It motivates me and I don't feel the slightest resentment because, you know, it's my goal to get to where they are."

And this is the answer from Colleen, a single mother of two who is usually direct and vivacious but now looks at some spot straight ahead of her, where perhaps the ancestor who escaped from the Great Potato Famine is staring back at her, as intent as I am on what she will say: "I don't mind, really, because I guess I'm a simple person, and I don't want what they have. I mean, it's nothing to me. But what I would like is to be able to take a day off now and then . . . if I had to . . . and still be able to buy groceries the next day."

I work one last day at the Woodcrest and then call in sick. Sorry, Linda, Pete, and all you sweet, demented old ladies! I visit Lori on Sunday and let her have the satisfaction of returning my uniforms to Ted and explaining my departure however she wants.

three

Selling in Minnesota

From the air Minnesota is the very perfection of early summer—the blue of the lakes merging with the blue of the sky, neatly sculpted clouds pasted here and there, strips of farmland in alternating chartreuse and emerald—a lush, gentle landscape, seemingly penetrable from any angle. I had thought for months of going to Sacramento or somewhere else in California's Central Valley not far from Berkeley, where I'd spent the spring. But warnings about the heat and the allergies put me off, not to mention my worry that the Latinos might be hogging all the crap jobs and substandard housing for themselves, as they so often do. Don't ask me why Minneapolis came to mind, maybe I just had a yearning for deciduous trees. It's a relatively liberal state, I knew that, and more merciful than many to its welfare poor. A half an hour or so of Web research revealed an agreeably tight labor market, with entry-level jobs advertised at $8 an hour or more and studio apartments for $400 or less. If some enterprising journalist wants to test the low-wage way of life in darkest Idaho or Louisiana, more power to her. Call me gutless, but what I was looking for this time around was a comfortable correspondence between income and rent, a few mild adventures, a soft landing.

I pick up my Rent-A-Wreck from a nice fellow—this must be the famous "Minnesota nice"—who volunteers the locations of NPR and classic rock on the radio. We agree that swing sucks and maybe would have discovered a few more points of convergence, only I'm on what a certain Key West rock jock likes to call "a mission from God." I've got my map of the Twin Cities area, purchased for $10 at the airport, and an apartment belonging to friends of a friend that I can use for a few days free of charge while they visit relatives back East. Well, not entirely free of charge, since the deal is I have to take care of their cockatiel, a caged bird that, for reasons of ornithological fitness and sanity, has to be let out of the cage for a few hours a day. I had agreed to this on the phone without thinking, only fully recalling, when I get to the apartment, that birds-at-close-range are one of the phobias I have always allowed myself, along with oversized moths and anything derived from oranges. I find the place with no trouble, delighted that the city and my map are in such perfect agreement, and spend an hour with one of my hosts absorbing cockatiel technology. At one point, my host lets the bird out of its cage and it flies directly at my face. With enormous effort, I bow my head and shut my eyes while it hops around on my hair, pecking and grooming.

Don't let the cockatiel throw you off; this is no yuppie ambience. It's a tiny, cluttered one-bedroom affair furnished by the Salvation Army and done up in late seventies graduate student décor. When my hosts leave, I find no olive oil or balsamic vinegar in the cupboards, no half-empty bottles of Chardonnay in the fridge, no alcohol at all other than a solidly blue-collar half-pint of Seagram's 7, and the favored spread is margarine. It's pleasant enough, even cozy, with a firm bed and views of a tree-lined street—except for the bird. But as I'd learned from my coworkers in Maine—several of whom had spent time in tightly shared space—people who depend on the generosity of others for their lodging always have something untoward to put up with, typically incompatible relatives and long waits for the bathroom. So let the cockatiel—Budgie, as I came to call him, instead of his more pretentious given name—be a stand-in in this story for the intrusive in-laws and noisy housemates that a person of limited means crashing with distant family in a strange city might normally expect to endure.

Never mind. I'm off first thing in the morning to look for a job. No waitressing, nursing homes, or housecleaning this time; I'm psyched for a change—retail, maybe, or factory work. I drive to the two nearest Wal-Marts, fill out applications, then head for a third one a forty-five-minute drive away on the opposite edge of the city. I drop off my application and am about to start hitting the Targets and Kmarts when I get an idea: no one is going to hire me based on an application showing no job experience—I have written, as usual, that I am a divorced homemaker reentering the workforce. What I have to do is make a personal appearance and exhibit my sunny, self-confident self. So I go to the pay phone in the front of the store, call the store's number, and ask for personnel. I'm put through to Roberta, who is impressed by my initiative and tells me I can come on in to her office in the back of the store. Roberta, a bustling platinum-haired woman of sixty or so, tells me there's nothing wrong with my "app"; she herself raised six children before starting at Wal-Mart, where she rose to her present position in just a few years, due mainly to the fact that she's a "people person." She can offer me a job now, but first a little "survey," on which there are no right or wrong answers, she assures me, just whatever I think. As it happens, I've already taken the Wal-Mart survey once, in Maine, and I rush through it again with aplomb. Roberta takes it off to another room, where, she says, a computer will "score" it. After about ten minutes, she's back with alarming news: I've gotten three answers wrong—well, not exactly *wrong* but in need of further discussion.

Now, my approach to preemployment personality tests has been zero tolerance vis-à-vis the obvious "crimes"—drug use and theft—but to leave a little wriggle room elsewhere, just so it doesn't look like I'm faking out the test. My approach was wrong. When presenting yourself as a potential employee, you can never be too much of a suck-up. Take the test proposition that "rules have to be followed to the letter at all times": I had agreed to this only "strongly" rather than "very strongly" or "totally" and now Roberta wants to know why. Well, rules have to be interpreted sometimes, I say, people have to use some discretion. Otherwise, why, you might as well have machines do all the work instead of actual human beings. She beams at this—"Discretion, very good!"—and jots something down. With my other wrong answers similarly accounted for, Roberta introduces me to "what Wal-Mart is all about." She personally read Sam Walton's book (his autobiography, *Made in America*) before starting to work here and found that the three pillars of Wal-Mart philosophy precisely fit her own, and these are service, excellence (or something like that), and she can't remember the third. Service, that's the key, helping people, solving their problems, helping them shop—and how do I feel about that? I testify to a powerful altruism in retail-related matters and even find myself getting a bit misty-eyed over this bond that I share with Roberta. All I have to do now is pass a drug test, which she schedules me to take at the beginning of next week.

If it weren't for the drug test, I might have stopped looking right then and there, but there has been a chemical indiscretion in recent weeks and I'm not at all sure I can pass. A poster in the room where Roberta interviewed me warns job applicants not to "waste your time or ours" if you've taken drugs within the last six weeks. If I had used cocaine or heroin there would be no problem, since these are water-soluble and wash out of the body in a couple of days. (LSD isn't even tested for.) But my indiscretion involved the only drug usually detected by testing, marijuana, which is fat-soluble and, I have read, can linger in the body for months. And what about the prescription drugs I've been taking for a chronic nasal congestion problem? What if Claritin-D, which gives you a nice little bounce, shows up as crystal meth?

So it's back to the car and my red-inked help-wanted ads, both in the *Star Tribune* and a throwaway called *Employment News*. I visit a couple of staffing agencies aimed at industrial jobs and certify that I have no physical limitations and can lift twenty pounds over my head, though I would feel better if I knew how many reps they have in mind. Then there's a long

drive to the other side of town, where I have an actual appointment for an interview for an assembly job. It's been a few years
since I engaged in urban highway driving, and I give myself
high grades for fearless and agile navigation, but eventually the
afternoon traffic defeats me. I can't find the factory, at least not
before 5:00 P.M., and pull into a shopping center parking lot to
find a way to get turned around. I find myself in front of a
Menards housewares store—a midwestern Home Depot–like
chain—and since a sign says, "Now Hiring," I might as well go
on in and put my confrontational strategy to the test again.
Wandering into the lumberyard behind the store, I flag down a
fellow identified as Raymond by his ID badge, who offers to
walk me to the personnel office. Is this a good place to work,
I want to know. He says that it's OK, it's just his second job
anyway, and that he doesn't get mad at the guests because it's
not his fault if the wood is crap. The guests? These must be the
customers, and I'm glad to have learned the term in advance so
I won't wince or gag in front of management.

Raymond drops me off with Paul, a thick-armed blond guy
who is, compared with Roberta, painfully short of people
skills. In response to my homemaking history, he mutters only,
"That doesn't bother me," and hands me the personality test.
This one is shorter than Wal-Mart's and apparently aimed at a
rougher crowd: Am I more or less likely than other people to
get into fistfights? Are there situations in which dealing cocaine
is not a crime? A long, repetitive stretch on stealing, featuring
variants on the question: "In the last year I have stolen (check
dollar amount below) worth of goods from my employers."
When I'm done, Paul eyeballs the test and barks out, "What
is your weakest point?" Uh, lack of experience—obviously.
"Do you take initiative?" I'm here, aren't I? I could have just

dropped off the application. So it's a go. Paul sees me in plumbing, $8.50 to start, drug screen results, of course, pending. I shake his hand to close the deal.[1]

Friday evening: I've been in Minneapolis for just over fifteen hours, driven from the southern suburbs to the northern ones, dropped off a half dozen apps, and undergone two face-to-face interviews. Job searches take their toll, even in the case of totally honest applicants, and I am feeling particularly damaged. The personality tests, for example: the truth is I don't much care if my fellow workers are getting high in the parking lot or even lifting the occasional retail item, and I certainly wouldn't snitch if I did. Nor do I believe that management rules by divine right or the undiluted force of superior knowledge, as the "surveys" demand you acknowledge. It whittles you down to lie up to fifty times in the space of the fifteen minutes or so it takes to do a "survey," even when there's a higher moral purpose to serve. Equally draining is the effort to look both perky and compliant at the same time, for half an hour or more at a stretch, because while you need to evince "initiative," you don't want to come across as someone who might initiate something like a union organizing drive. Then there is the threat of the drug tests, hanging over me like a fast-approaching SAT. It rankles—at some deep personal, physical level—to know that the many engaging qualities I believe I

[1] The St. Paul–based Jobs Now Coalition estimated that, in 1997, a "living wage" for a single parent supporting a single child in the Twin Cities metro area was $11.77 an hour. This estimate was based on monthly expenses that included $266 for food (all meals cooked and eaten at home), $261 for child care, and $550 for rent ("The Cost of Living in Minnesota: A Report by the Jobs Now Coalition on the Minimum Cost of Basic Needs for Minnesota Families in 1997"). No one has updated this "living wage" to take into account the accelerating Twin Cities rent inflation of 2000 (see page 140).

have to offer—friendliness, reliability, willingness to learn—can all be trumped by my pee.[2]

In a spirit of contrition for multiple sins, I decide to devote the weekend to detox. A Web search reveals that I am on a heavily traveled path; there are dozens of sites offering help to the would-be drug-test passer, mostly in the form of ingestible products, though one site promises to send a vial of pure, drug-free urine, battery-heated to body temperature. Since I don't have time to order and receive any drug-test-evasion products, I linger over a site in which hundreds of letters, typically with subject lines reading "Help!!! Test in Three Days!!!" are soberly answered by "Alec." Here I learn that my leanness is an advantage—there aren't too many places for the cannabis derivatives to hide out in—and that the only effective method is to flush the damn stuff out with massive quantities of fluid, at least three gallons a day. To hurry the process, there is a product called CleanP supposedly available at GNC, so I drive fifteen minutes to the nearest one, swigging tap water from an Evian bottle all the way, and ask the kid manning the place where his,

---

[2] There are many claims for workplace drug testing: supposedly, it results in reduced rates of accidents and absenteeism, fewer claims on health insurance plans, and increased productivity. However, none of these claims has been substantiated, according to a 1999 report from the American Civil Liberties Union, "Drug Testing: A Bad Investment." Studies show that preemployment testing does not lower absenteeism, accidents, or turnover and (at least in the high-tech workplaces studied) actually lowered productivity—presumably due to its negative effect on employee morale. Furthermore, the practice is quite costly. In 1990, the federal government spent $11.7 million to test 29,000 federal employees. Since only 153 tested positive, the cost of detecting a single drug user was $77,000. Why do employers persist in the practice? Probably in part because of advertising by the roughly $2 billion drug-testing industry, but I suspect that the demeaning effect of testing may also hold some attraction for employers.

uh, detox products are kept. Maybe he's used to a stream of momlike women demanding CleanP, because he leads me poker-faced to an impressively large locked glass case—locked either because the average price of GNC's detox products is $49.95 or because the market is thought to consist of desperate and not particularly law-abiding individuals. I read the ingredients and buy two of them separately—creatinine and a diuretic called uva ursis—for a total of $30. So here is the program: drink water at all times, along with frequent doses of diuretic, and (this is my own scientific contribution) avoid salt in any form at all since salt encourages water retention, meaning no processed foods, fast foods, or condiments of any kind. If I want that job in plumbing at Menards, I have to make myself into an unobstructed pipe: water in and water just as pure and drinkable coming out.

My other task for Saturday is to find a place to live. I go through all the apartment-finding agencies in the phone book—Apartment Mart, Apartment Search, Apartments Available, and so on—and leave messages. I also try all the apartment buildings listed, finding, at the two buildings where someone actually answers, that they want twelve-month leases. I walk to the supermarket to pick up the Sunday paper, pausing to apply for a job while I'm there. Yes, they could use someone; things get pretty hectic around the first of the month, right after the welfare checks go out; I can come back next week. The newspaper, though, is a disappointment. There is exactly one furnished studio apartment listed for the entire Twin Cities area, and they're not answering the phone on the weekend. Maybe, though, given the incipient incontinence induced by the flush-out regimen, it's just as well I have no apartments to see. Dinner is a quarter of a BBQ chicken from the supermarket, unsalted and washed down with a familiar, low-tech diuretic—beer.

This is not, all things considered, my finest hour. If I could just surrender to my increasingly aqueous condition and wait out the weekend with a novel, things would be looking up. But home in this instance is not a restful place; it's more like what is known in the military as a "situation." When I am home, Budgie wants to be out of his cage, a desire he makes known by squawking or, what is far worse, by pacing dementedly. When he is out of his cage, he wants to sit on my head and worry my hair and my glasses frames. To minimize the damage, I don't let him out unless I am wearing my hooded sweatshirt, tied up tight enough to cover my hair and most of my face, and still I am constantly having to move him from his favorite face-to-face perch on my shoulder to, say, my forearm, from which he will work his way ineluctably back to my face. This is what anyone coming to the door would encounter: a cringing figure, glasses peering out the porthole of her sweatshirt, topped by a large, crested—and, I can only imagine, quite pleased with its dominant position—exotic white bird. But I cannot incarcerate him nearly as much as I would like to. It's my job—isn't it?—my way of earning my shelter, to be this creature's friend and surrogate flock.

Unfortunately, Budgie does not serve the same functions for me, and on Sunday I decide to seek out my own kind. A New York friend, a young African American feminist, had urged me to look up her aunt in Minneapolis, and I have a reason beyond sociability for doing so: I have been worrying that the scenario I have created for myself, both here and in Maine, is totally artificial. Who, in real life, plops herself down in a totally strange environment—without housing, family connections, or job—and attempts to become a viable resident? Well, it turns out that my friend's aunt did exactly that in the early nineties: got on a Greyhound bus in New York, with two children in tow, disembarking in the utterly strange state of Florida. This is a story I have to hear, so I call and get a wary invitation to come on over this afternoon. Caroline, as I'll call her, is a commanding presence, with high cheekbones and quick-moving, shamanistic eyes. She gets me my drink du jour—water—introduces me to her children, and explains that it's her husband's day off, which he is spending upstairs in bed. The house—well, she apologizes for it, though three bedrooms in a freestanding building for $825 a month doesn't seem so bad to me at the moment. She itemizes its deficiencies: the bedrooms are tiny; the block is infested with drug dealers; the dining room ceiling leaks whenever the bathroom above it is used; the toilet can be flushed only by pouring in a bucket of water. And why are they here? Because on her $9 an hour as an assistant bookkeeper at a downtown hotel, plus her husband's $10 as a maintenance worker, minus utilities and $59 a week for health insurance (she is diabetic, the five-year-old asthmatic), this is what you get. Yet if you do the arithmetic, these people are earning nearly $40,000 a year, which makes them officially "middle class."

I explain my mission in Minneapolis, although it turns out her niece has already briefed her, and ask her to tell me about her move to Florida ten years ago. This is the story more or less as it emerged, since she didn't mind my taking notes, of someone doing in real life what I am doing only in the service of journalism:

She had been living in New Jersey, working at a bank, when she decided to leave her husband because he "wasn't involved" with the children. She moved in with her mother in Queens but found it impossible to get to her job in New Jersey from there, in addition to taking her youngest child to day care every morning. Then her brother moved in, so you had three adults and two children in a two-bedroom apartment, which was just not working out. So she decided to take off for Florida, where she had heard the rents were lower. What she had was their clothes, the Greyhound tickets, and $1,600 in cash. That was all. They got off the bus in a town a little south of Orlando, and here a nice cab driver—she still remembers his name—took them to a low-priced hotel. The next step was to find a church: "Always find a church." People from the church drove her around to the WIC office (Women, Infants, and Children, a federal program offering food help to pregnant women and mothers of young children) and to find a school for her twelve-year-old girl and day care for the baby. Sometimes they also helped with groceries. Soon Caroline got a job cleaning hotel rooms—twenty-eight to thirty rooms a day for $2–$3 a room, for a total of about $300 a week. It was "go to bed with a back-ache and wake up with a backache." The little girl had to pick up the baby at day care and watch him until Caroline got home at about 8:00 P.M., which means she didn't get much chance to go outside and play.

What was it like to start all over in a completely new place? "Anxiety attack! You know what I'm saying?" It was the stress, she thinks, that gave her diabetes. There she was—thirsty all the time, blurry vision, a terrible itching of her privates—and she had no idea what the symptoms meant. One doctor told her it had to be an STD, but it had been a long, long time since any sex had occurred. One morning the Lord told her, "Go to a hospital. Walk, don't ride." She walked thirty blocks and passed out at the hospital. Maybe the Lord wanted her to walk so she'd pass out and finally get some attention.

There were good things that happened, though. She used to help a man at the hotel where she cleaned, a man who was sick with cancer, bringing him food and even cleaning the bad-smelling sores, and he was so grateful that he once gave her $325, which he knew was the exact amount of her rent. And there was one major friend, Irene, whom Caroline met "at a Dumpster." Irene had problems, yes. She was both black and Indian, a migrant farmworker, and had been raped by someone and also abused by her boyfriend, who left an ugly scar on her face. The boyfriend found the rapist and hacked him to death and ended up permanently in prison. So Caroline took Irene in and for a while it worked out very well. Irene got a job at Taco Bell and helped with the kids, whom she fussed over and loved as her own. Then Irene started drinking and "dancing on chairs" in bars, finally leaving to live with a man. Caroline misses her and even went back to Florida once to try to find her. She could have died. One time a cancer the size of a quarter popped out of her right nipple. It's hard not knowing.

It was in Florida that Caroline met the current husband, a white man, as it turns out, and her tribulations did not end with marriage but went on to include bouts of homelessness and a lot more interstate travel by Greyhound with children. When, after two hours, I get up to go, Caroline asks if I'm a vegetarian. I apologize for not being one, and she rushes into the kitchen, coming back with a family-sized container of her homemade chicken stew, which I accept with heartfelt gratitude: dinner. We hug. She walks me to my car and we hug again. So I have a friend now in Minneapolis, and the odd thing is that she is the original—the woman who uprooted herself and came out somehow on her feet and who did all this in real life and with children—while I am the imitation, the pallid, child-free pretender.

BUT ON TUESDAY, WHEN THE POST–MEMORIAL DAY WEEK BEGINS, my life seems real enough again in a gray and baleful way. This is my day of drug tests, also of traffic and a steady, appropriately sphincter-relaxing rain. The first test, for Wal-Mart, is painless enough, conducted at a chiropractor's office a few miles down the highway from Wal-Mart itself. I'm given two plastic containers—one to pee into and one to hold the decanted sample—and sent down the hall to an ordinary public rest room. Easy enough to substitute someone else's pee, if I'd had a vial of it in my pocket or met a potential donor in the rest room. The next test, for Menards, takes me to the southwestern suburbs, to a regular allopathic hospital, complete with patients being whisked around corridors on gurneys. A dozen people are already ahead of me in the waiting room of the SmithKline Beecham suite I've been sent to, most of them, judging from the usual class cues, of the low-wage variety. The waiting room TV is tuned to Robin Givens's talk show *Forgive or Forget,* where today's theme is "You took me in and I cleaned you out." Seems eighteen-year-old Cory stole from the cousin who took him in, thus ruining Christmas for the cousin's girlfriend and her child. Cory is not repentant, in fact makes excuses about having had to cheat and steal all the way up from the projects, that's how his life has been. Robin beats the air with her fists and yells, "Cory, Cory, stop being a *victim!*" Thievery is nothing, apparently, compared to the crime of victimhood. With each fresh denunciation of Cory, the studio audience applauds more excitedly. He is bad, as are some of the impassive viewers right in this room, who will soon be judged and exposed by their urine. My mind slides back to one of the "approve/disapprove" statements on the Wal-Mart survey: "There is room in every corporation for a nonconformist." But no, no, no! The correct answer, as we will all find out soon enough, is "totally disagree."

Finally, after forty minutes, I am called out of the waiting room by an officious woman in blue scrubs. What are they planning—to cut out my bladder if I fail to produce a testable volume of pee? I ask whether they do anything but drug testing here. No, that's pretty much it. She checks my photo ID, then squirts what looks like soap onto my palms, although there is no sink in evidence. Now I'm to go into a bathroom and wash with water while she waits, leaving my purse with her. I pause for a beat or two, goo-filled hands held out, pondering the issues of trust that have arisen between her and me. Why, for example, am I supposed to leave her with my purse while she doesn't even trust me not to sprinkle some drug-dissolving substance into my urine? But for all I know, any display of attitude might lead her to slant the results. So I go meekly into the rest room, wash my hands, and then pee, which I am allowed to do with the door shut, and our little parody of medical care is complete. The whole venture, including drive time and wait, has taken an hour and forty minutes, about what it took for the Wal-Mart test, and it occurs to me that one of the effects of drug testing is to limit worker mobility—maybe even one of the *functions*. Each potential new job requires (1) the application, (2) the interview, and (3) the drug test—which is something to ponder with gasoline running at nearly two dollars a gallon, not to mention what you may have to pay for a babysitter.

Until I know the drug test results, I feel obliged to keep looking for jobs. Most of my encounters are predictable and unpromising—fill out the app, get told to wait for a call, etc.— but one stands out from the corporate, legalistic, euphemistic, and thoroughly aboveboard feel of all the others. The ad is for "customer service" work, a type of job I tend to avoid because it normally involves a résumé, which in turn would involve levels of prevarication I am not prepared to attempt. But this customer service job is described as "entry-level." When I call I am told to come in at three sharp and to be sure to "dress professional." The latter injunction presents a challenge, since my wardrobe consists of T-shirts and only two pairs of pants other than blue jeans, but I have a jacket and decent shoes brought along for a stop in New York on the way to Minneapolis, and this, fortified with lipstick and knee-highs, makes for a pretty damn impressive getup, I think. When I arrive at Mountain Air (as we'll call it), in a characterless white box building just off a service road, nine other applicants are already waiting. It turns out this is a group interview, conducted by Todd in a large room, where we applicants sit in folding chairs while Todd, a sharply dressed fellow of about thirty, lectures and shows transparencies.

Todd speaks very rapidly in a singsong cadence, suggesting that he does this several times a day. Mountain Air, he says, is an "environmental consulting firm" offering help to people with asthma and allergies as a "free service." We will be sent out to the sufferers in our own cars, making $1,650 if we complete fifty-four two-hour appointments in thirty days—though you'd have to be pretty lazy to make only that much. Plus there are incredible perks like weekend training sessions held all over the country where they "get stuff done, of course, like hearing motivational speakers, but you can bring your spouse and have a great time." All we have to be is eighteen or older, bondable, possessing a car and a home phone and having one year of Minnesota residency. Whoops! He asks if any of us are not long-term Minnesota residents, and when I raise my hand he says the requirement can sometimes be waived. What Mountain Air is really looking for is—and here he reads from a transparency— "Self-disciplined/Money-motivated/Positive attiude."

Nothing, I note, about providing a service or healing the sick. In fact, compared with Wal-Mart's unctuous service ethic, Todd's emphasis on the bottom line is positively refreshing. We will be independent contractors, he tells us, not employees, which means, "if you lie to a customer the company is not responsible." Even, I wonder, if the lies are part of the sales pitch the company has taught you? It's very simple, Todd assures us, just a "matter of taking people who have a very serious problem, though probably not anywhere near as serious as they think it is, and leaving them happy." Any questions? None of this has made any sense to me at all, but I limit myself to asking what the product is, assuming there is some kind of product involved. Todd opens a cardboard box that I had not noticed sitting on the floor near his feet: a squat, slightly menacing-looking appliance he introduces as the "Filter Queen." "So this is a selling job?" someone asks. "No," Todd says with some vehemence. "We have a product and if they want it we give it to them"—though he can't mean give it to them for free. Now we are to have our personal three-minute interviews. When my turn comes, he asks why I want to do this and I say something, without thinking, about wanting to help people with asthma. Where do I think I am, Wal-Mart? Because when I call at the designated time two hours later, I'm told there's no job for me now, although I have made it to the waiting list. Maybe it was the residency issue that did me in, though I suspect it was the misplaced hypocrisy.

Meanwhile, there is the increasingly desperate apartment search. Whatever else I am doing at any point in this story, you need to picture me waiting for a call or looking for a chance to call some rental agency for a second or third or fourth time. Now that we're into the weekdays I sometimes get live humans on the other end of the line, but they are disdainful or discouraging. One directs me to a throwaway apartment directory available in boxes on the sidewalk, but its offerings all include hot tubs and on-site gyms and go for over $1,000 a month. Another tells me that I've picked a bad time to come to Minneapolis; the vacancy rate is less than 1 percent, and if we're talking about *affordable*— why, it might be as low as a tenth of that. Listings in the *Star Tribune* are meager or nonexistent. No one returns my calls. Besides, it is dawning on me belatedly that Minneapolis is far vaster than Key West or Portland, Maine, and that my two live job possibilities—Wal-Mart and Menards—are separated by about thirty miles. My appetite for navigating the Twin Cities highways has been dwindling rapidly. Everywhere I go, some fellow or other who has never heard of Minnesota nice is stalking me in his pickup truck, making me covet the bumper sticker I see more than once: "If you're not a hemorrhoid, get off my ass." Nor is the leading classic rock station turning out to be sufficiently supportive. I can handle seventy-five-mile-per-hour tailgaters on Creedence Clearwater Revival or even ZZ Top, but the Eagles and the Doobie Brothers are just no help. So one thing I do not want is to live at a hair-raising distance from my job, assuming, of course, that I get a job.

There is one possibility—one place in the entire Twin Cities that rents "affordable" furnished apartments on a weekly or monthly basis—and this place, the Hopkins Park Plaza, becomes the focus of my residential yearnings for the next three weeks, my personal Shangri-La. On my third call (the first two calls were not returned), I reach Hildy, who doesn't think there's anything at the moment, but I might as well come out and pay the application fee, which is $20 in cash. When I find the couple of two-story brick buildings that constitute the Park Plaza, several other apartment seekers—a middle-aged white guy with auburn dyed hair, a young Hispanic man (it's Latino in California, Hispanic here), an older white woman—are waiting for Hildy too, which explains why she doesn't return calls: the market is entirely on her side. The place, when I finally get taken around by Hildy, seems OK, although the corridors tend to be dark, noisy, and permeated with kitchen-waste smells. I can have a room without a kitchenette right now if I want, but it's in the basement and the price—$144 a week—seems a little steep. So I decide to wait for one with a kitchenette to open up—any day now, Hildy assures me, turnover is dependably high. This seems like a prudent and thrifty decision at the moment, but it turns out to be a major mistake.

I decide there must be something I am doing wrong, some cue I am missing. Budgie's owners had been confident that Apartment Search would find me a place. When I call another friend of a friend, a professor at a college in St. Paul who has briefed me on the Twin Cities' industrial history, he concedes to being aware of an affordable-housing "crisis" but has no idea what I should do. Those rental agents who are kind

enough to talk to me all recommend the same thing: find a
motel that rents by the week and stay there until something
opens up.[3] So, through multiple calls, I arrive at a list of eleven
motels in the Twin Cities area, all of them of the non-brand-
name variety, offering weekly rates. The rates, though, are not
anybody's definition of "affordable," ranging from $200 a
week at the Hill View in Shakopee to $295 at the Twin Lakes in
southern Minneapolis, and many of these places are full. I head
for the Hill View, which wants a $60 cash deposit. I drive and I
drive. I go off the map, I leave suburbs and commercial strips
far behind, I enter the open fields, which make for a nice
change, drivingwise—but to live in? The vicinity of the Hill
View contains no diners, no fast-food joints or grocery stores,
no commercial establishments at all except for a couple of
agricultural-equipment warehouses. The distance is unaccept-
able; as is the room, when I get to see it: no microwave, no
fridge, hardly any space not occupied by the bed. And what

[3] The last few years have seen a steady decline in the number of affordable
apartments nationwide. In 1991 there were forty-seven affordable rental units
available to every one hundred low-income families, while by 1997 there were
only thirty-six such units for every one hundred families ("Rental Housing
Assistance—The Worsening Crisis: A Report to Congress on Worst-Case
Housing Needs," Housing and Urban Development Department, March
2000). No national—or even reliable local—statistics are available, but apparently more and more of the poor have been reduced to living in motels. Census
takers distinguish between standard motels, such as those that tourists stay in,
and residential motels, which rent on a weekly basis, usually to long-term ten-
ants. But many motels contain mixed populations or change from one type to
the other depending on the season. Long-term motel residents are almost certainly undercounted, since motel owners often deny access to census takers
and the residents themselves may be reluctant to admit they live in motels,
crowded in with as many as four people or more in a room (Willoughby Mari-
ano, "The Inns and Outs of the Census," *Los Angeles Times,* May 22, 2000).

would I do if I didn't feel like being in bed—invite myself in for a tour of the Caterpillar parts warehouse?

Twin Lakes (not its real name) is at least in Minneapolis. There the East Indian owner tells me that all his residents are long-term, working people and that I can have a room on the second floor, where I won't have to keep the drapes shut during the day for privacy. Again, no fridge or microwave. Weakly, I tell him I'll take it and will move in in a couple of days. No problem. He even waives the deposit. But I have a bad feeling about the place, partly because everything looks gray and stained and partly because there's a deranged-looking guy hanging out by the coin-op washer-dryer who follows me with bloodshot blue eyes.

On the job front, though, things are moving along briskly. I had been told at Menards to show up for "orientation" at ten o'clock Wednesday morning, and since I assume that my being hired is conditional on passing the drug test, I call to confirm the appointment. Yes, they're expecting me—I hope not just for the purpose of denouncing me as a chemical misfit. But the orientation is friendly and upbeat. Lee-Ann, a worn-looking blonde in her forties, and I sit across a table from Walt, who lays out the main points in a jolly, offhand way: Be nice to the guests, even when they get irate because they can't return things, and they're always trying to return things. Don't be absent without calling in. Watch out for a certain top manager, who hits on women when he visits the store and generally acts like "a shit." We will need to wear belts, to which a knife (for opening cardboard boxes, I suppose) and a tape measure will be attached, and the cost of these items, which he pushes across the table to us, will be deducted from our first paycheck. And oh yes, we will be getting "little presents" now and then—

ballpoint pens, coffee mugs, T-shirts promoting seasonal items. Then Walt hands us our vests and our ID badges, and I am touched to see that he has made up two for me, one with "Barbara" and another with "Barb." I can take my choice.

When Walt leaves the room for a moment, I turn to Lee-Ann and say, "Does this mean we're hired?" Because it seems odd to me that no offer has been made or accepted. "Looks like," she says, and tells me that she hasn't even taken her drug test. She went to the testing place, but she didn't have any photo ID because her wallet was stolen, and of course they wouldn't test her without photo ID. Then Walt comes back and takes me out on the floor to meet Steve, a "really great guy," who will be my supervisor in plumbing. But here, on the sales floor, doubt rushes in. The shelves of plumbing equipment, and there seem to be acres of them, contain not a single item I can name, which gives me an idea of what it feels like to be aphasic. Would I be able to get by with pointing and grunting? Steve's smile seems more like a smirk, as if he's reading my mind and finding not a speck of plumbing knowledge lodged within it. Start Friday, he says, shift is noon to eleven. I think I haven't heard him right, nor can I quite believe the wage Walt tells me I'll be getting—not $8.50 but an incredible $10 an hour.

Now I don't need Wal-Mart anymore, I think, although it turns out they need me. Roberta calls to tell me, in fulsome tones, that my "drug screen is fine" and that I'm due in tomorrow at three for orientation. The test result does not have the desired effect of making me feel absolved or even clean. In fact I feel irritated and can't help wondering whether I could have gotten the same result without spending $30 and three days on detox and bloat. I ask her what the pay is—it should be noted that she does not offer this information herself—and when she says $7 an hour, I think: OK, case closed. But I decide, in the spirit of caution and inquiry, to attend the Wal-Mart orientation anyway. This turns out, for unforeseen physiological reasons, to be another major mistake.

For sheer grandeur, scale, and intimidation value, I doubt if any corporate orientation exceeds that of Wal-Mart. I have been told that the process will take eight hours, which will include two fifteen-minute breaks and one half-hour break for a meal, and will be paid for like a regular shift. When I arrive, dressed neatly in khakis and clean T-shirt, as befits a potential Wal-Mart "associate," I find there are ten new hires besides myself, mostly young and Caucasian, and a team of three, headed by Roberta, to do the "orientating." We sit around a long table in the same windowless room where I was interviewed, each with a thick folder of paperwork in front of us, and hear Roberta tell once again about raising six children, being a "people person," discovering that the three principles of Wal-Mart philosophy were the same as her own, and so on. We begin with a video, about fifteen minutes long, on the history and philosophy of Wal-Mart, or, as an anthropological observer might call it, the Cult of Sam. First young Sam Walton, in uniform, comes back from the war. He starts a store, a sort of five-and-dime; he marries and fathers four attractive children; he receives a Medal of Freedom from President Bush, after which he promptly dies, making way for the eulogies. But the company goes on, yes indeed. Here the arc of the story soars upward unstoppably, pausing only to mark some fresh milestone of corporate expansion. 1992: Wal-Mart becomes the largest retailer in the world. 1997: Sales top $100 billion. 1998: The number of Wal-Mart associates hits 825,000, making Wal-Mart the largest private employer in the nation.

Each landmark date is accompanied by a clip showing throngs of shoppers, swarms of associates, or scenes of handsome new stores and their adjoining parking lots. Over and over we hear in voiceover or see in graphic display the "three principles," which are maddeningly, even defiantly, nonparallel: "respect for the individual, exceeding customers' expectations, strive for excellence."

"Respect for the individual" is where we, the associates, come in, because vast as Wal-Mart is, and tiny as we may be as individuals, everything depends on us. Sam always said, and is shown saying, that "the best ideas come from the associates"— for example, the idea of having a "people greeter," an elderly employee (excuse me, associate) who welcomes each customer as he or she enters the store. Three times during the orientation, which began at three and stretches to nearly eleven, we are reminded that this brainstorm originated in a mere associate, and who knows what revolutions in retailing each one of us may propose? Because our ideas are welcome, more than welcome, and we are to think of our managers not as bosses but as "servant leaders," serving us as well as the customers. Of course, all is not total harmony, in every instance, between associates and their servant-leaders. A video on "associate honesty" shows a cashier being caught on videotape as he pockets some bills from the cash register. Drums beat ominously as he is led away in handcuffs and sentenced to four years.

The theme of covert tensions, overcome by right thinking and positive attitude, continues in the twelve-minute video entitled *You've Picked a Great Place to Work*. Here various associates testify to the "essential feeling of family for which Wal-Mart is so well-known," leading up to the conclusion that we don't need a union. Once, long ago, unions had a place in

American society, but they "no longer have much to offer workers," which is why people are leaving them "by the droves."
Wal-Mart is booming; unions are declining: judge for yourself.
But we are warned that "unions have been targeting Wal-Mart
for years." Why? For the dues money of course. Think of what
you would lose with a union: first, your dues money, which
could be $20 a month "and sometimes much more." Second,
you would lose "your voice" because the union would insist on
doing your talking for you. Finally, you might lose even your
wages and benefits because they would all be "at risk on the
bargaining table." You have to wonder—and I imagine some
of my teenage fellow orientees may be doing so—why such
fiends as these union organizers, such outright extortionists,
are allowed to roam free in the land.

There is more, much more than I could ever absorb, even if
it were spread out over a semester-long course. On the reason-
able assumption that none of us is planning to go home and
curl up with the "Wal-Mart Associate Handbook," our trainers start reading it out loud to us, pausing every few paragraphs
to ask, "Any questions?" There never are. Barry, the seventeen-
year-old to my left, mutters that his "butt hurts." Sonya, the
tiny African American woman across from me, seems frozen in
terror. I have given up on looking perky and am fighting to
keep my eyes open. No nose or other facial jewelry, we learn;
earrings must be small and discreet, not dangling; no blue jeans
except on Friday, and then you have to pay $1 for the privilege
of wearing them. No "grazing," that is, eating from food packages that somehow become open; no "time theft." This last
sends me drifting off in a sci-fi direction: *And as the time thieves
headed back to the year 3420, loaded with weekends and days off
looted from the twenty-first century* . . . Finally, a question. The

old guy who is being hired as a people greeter wants to know, "What is time theft?" Answer: Doing anything other than working during company time, anything at all. Theft of *our* time is not, however, an issue. There are stretches amounting to many minutes when all three of our trainers wander off, leaving us to sit there in silence or take the opportunity to squirm. Or our junior trainers go through a section of the handbook, and then Roberta, returning from some other business, goes over the same section again. My eyelids droop and I consider walking out. I have seen time move more swiftly during seven-hour airline delays. In fact, I am getting nostalgic about seven-hour airline delays. At least you can read a book or get up and walk around, take a leak.

On breaks, I drink coffee purchased at the Radio Grill, as the in-house fast-food place is called, the real stuff with caffeine, more because I'm concerned about being alert for the late-night drive home than out of any need to absorb all the Wal-Mart trivia coming my way. Now, here's a drug the drug warriors ought to take a little more interest in. Since I don't normally drink it at all—iced tea can usually be counted on for enough of a kick—the coffee has an effect like reagent-grade Dexedrine: my pulse races, my brain overheats, and the result in this instance is a kind of delirium. I find myself overly challenged by the little kindergarten-level tasks we are now given to do, such as affixing my personal bar code to my ID card, then sticking on the punch-out letters to spell my name. The letters keep curling up and sticking to my fingers, so I stop at "Barb," or more precisely, "BARB," drifting off to think of all the people I know who have gentrified their names in recent years—Patsy to Patricia, Dick to Richard, and so forth—while I am going in the other direction. Now we start taking turns going to the computers to begin our CBL, or Computer-Based Learning, and I become transfixed by the HIV-inspired module entitled "Bloodborne Pathogens," on what to do in the event that pools of human blood should show up on the sales floor. All right, you put warning cones around the puddles, don protective gloves, etc., but I can't stop trying to envision the circumstances in which these pools might arise: an associate uprising? a guest riot? I have gone through six modules, three more than we are supposed to do tonight—the rest are to be done in our spare moments over the next few weeks—when one of the trainers gently pries me away from the computer. We are allowed now to leave.

There follows the worst of many sleepless nights to come. On the drive home along the interstate, a guy doing over eighty passes me on the right at a few angstroms' distance, making the point that any highway has far more exits than you can see, infinitely many—final exits, that is. At this hour, which is nearly midnight, it takes me fifteen minutes to find a parking place, and another five to walk to the apartment, where I find that Budgie, distraught by my long absence, has gone totally postal. Feathers litter the floor under his cage, and he refuses to return to it even after a generous forty-five minutes of head time. I want to be fresh for my first day in plumbing tomorrow—Menards is still my choice—but a lot of small things have been going wrong, and at this level of finances, nothing wrong is ever quite small enough. My watch battery ran out and I had to spend $11 to get it replaced. My khakis developed a prominent ink stain that took three wash cycles ($3.75) and a treatment with Shout Gel ($1.29) to remove. There was the $20 application fee at the Park Plaza, plus $20 for the belt I need for Menards, purchased only after comparison shopping at a consignment store. And why hadn't I asked what that knife and tape measure are going to cost? I discover that the phone is no longer taking incoming calls or recording voice mail, so who knows what housing opportunities I have missed. Around two in the morning, I pop a Unisom to counteract the still-raging caffeine, but at five Budgie takes his revenge, greeting the prospect of dawn, which is still comfortably remote, with a series of scandalized squawks.

I am due at Menards at noon. At this point, although I have not formally accepted either job, I realize I am officially employed at both places, Wal-Mart and Menards. Maybe I'll combine both jobs or just blow off Wal-Mart and go for the better money at Menards. But Wal-Mart, with its endless orientation, has, alas, already sunk its talons into me. People working more than one job—and in effect I would be doing that for a day by going from my three-to-eleven stint at Wal-Mart to a day at Menards—have to take sleep deprivation in stride. I do not. I am shaky, my brain fried like that egg in the Partnership for a Drug-Free America commercial. How am I going to master the science of plumbing products when I can barely summon the concentration required to assemble a breakfast of peanut butter and toast? The world is coming at me in high-contrast snapshots, deprived of narrative continuity. I call Menards and get Paul on the line to clear up what exactly my shift is supposed to be. Steve—or was it Walt?—said noon till eleven, but that would be eleven hours, right?

"Right," he says. "You want to be full-time, don't you?"

And you're going to pay me ten dollars an hour?

"Ten dollars?" Paul asks, "Who told you ten?" He'll have to check on that; it can't be right.

Now thoroughly unnerved, I tell him I'm not working an

eleven-hour shift, not without time and a half after eight. I don't tell him about the generations of workers who fought and sometimes died for the ten-hour day and then the eight, although this is very much on my mind.[4] I just tell him I'm going to send my knife, my vest, and my tape measure back. In the days that follow I will try to rationalize this decision by telling myself that, given Wal-Mart's position as the nation's largest private employer, whatever I experience there will at least be of grand social significance. But this is just a way of prettifying yet another dumb mistake, the one involving all that coffee. The embarrassing truth is that I am just too exhausted to work, especially for eleven hours in a row.

Why hadn't I asked all these questions about wages and hours before? For that matter, why hadn't I bargained with Roberta when she called to tell me I'd passed the drug test— told her $7 an hour would be fine, as long as the benefits included a free lakeside condo with hot tub? At least part of the answer, which I only figured out weeks later, lies in the employers' deft handling of the hiring process. First you are an applicant, then suddenly you are an orientee. You're handed the application form and, a few days later, you're being handed the uniform and warned against nose rings and stealing. There's no intermediate point in the process in which you confront the potential employer as a free agent, entitled to cut her own deal. The intercalation of the drug test between application and hiring tilts the playing field even further, establishing that you, and not the employer, are the one who has something to

---

[4] Under the Fair Labor Standards Act it is in fact illegal not to pay time and a half for hours worked above forty hours a week. Certain categories of workers—professionals, managers, and farmworkers—are not covered by the FLSA, but retail workers are not among them.

prove. Even in the tightest labor market—and it doesn't get any tighter than Minneapolis, where I would probably have been welcome to apply at any commercial establishment I entered—the person who has precious labor to sell can be made to feel one down, way down, like a supplicant with her hand stretched out.

IT'S SATURDAY AND THE TIME HAS COME TO LEAVE MY FREE LODGINGS and neurotic avian roommate. A few hours before my hosts are scheduled to return, I pack up and head down to Twin Lakes, where—no big surprise—I find out that all the second-story rooms have been taken. The particular room I'd requested, which looks out on a backyard instead of a parking lot, is now occupied by a woman with a child, the owner tells me, and he is good enough to feel uncomfortable about asking them to move to a smaller one. So I decide that this is my out and call another weekly rental place on my list, the Clearview Inn (not its real name), which has two big advantages: it's about a twenty-minute drive from my Wal-Mart, as opposed to at least forty-five in the case of Twin Lakes, and the weekly rate is $245, compared to $295. This is still scandalously high, higher in fact than my aftertax weekly pay will amount to. But in our latest conversation Hildy has promised me a room with kitchenette by the end of next week, and I am confident I can get a weekend job at the supermarket I applied to, in bakery if I am lucky.

To say that some place is the worst motel in the country is, of course, to set oneself up for considerable challenge.[5] I have

[5] I may have to withdraw my claim. Until it was closed for fire code violations in 1997, the Parkway Motel in southern Maryland boasted exposed electrical wires, holes in room doors, and raw sewage on bathroom floors. But if price is entered into the competition, the Clearview Inn may still win, since the Park-

encountered plenty of contenders in my own travels—the one in Cleveland that turned into a brothel at night, the one in Butte where the window looked out into another room. Still, the Clearview Inn leaves the competition in the dust. I slide $255 in cash (the extra $10 is for telephone service) under the glass window that separates me from the young East Indian owner—East Indians seem to have a lock on the midwestern motel business—and am taken by his wife to a room memorable only for its overwhelming stench of mold. I don't have enough Claritin-D for this situation, a point I have to make by holding my nose, since her English does not extend to the concept of allergy. Air freshener? she suggests when she catches my meaning. Incense? There is a better room, her husband says when we return to the office, but—and here he fixes me with a narrow-eyed stare—I'd better not "trash" it. I attempt a reassuring chuckle, but the warning rankles for days: have I been fooling myself all these years, thinking I look like a mature and sober person when in fact anyone can see I'm a vandal?

Room 133 contains a bed, a chair, a chest of drawers, and a TV fastened to the wall. I plead for and get a lamp to supplement the single overhead bulb. Instead of the mold smell, I now breathe a mixture of fresh paint and what I eventually identify as mouse droppings. But the real problems are all window- and door-related: the single small window has no screen, and the room has no AC or fan. The curtain is transparently thin; the door has no bolt. Without a screen, the window should be sensibly closed at night, meaning no air, unless I'm

---

way was charging only $20 a day at the time (Todd Shields, "Charles Cracks Down on Dilapidated Motels," *Washington Post,* April 20, 1997).

willing to take my chances with the bugs and the neighbors. Who are the neighbors? The motel forms a toilet-seat shape around the parking lot, and I can see an inexplicable collection. A woman with a baby in her arms leans in the doorway of one room. Two bunches of teenagers, one group black and the other white, seem to share adjoining rooms. There are several unencumbered men of various ages, including an older white man in work clothes whose bumper sticker says, "Don't steal, the government hates competition"—as if the income tax were the only thing keeping him from living at the Embassy Suites right now. When it gets dark I go outside and look through my curtain, and yes, you can see pretty much everything, at least in silhouette. I eat the deli food I've brought with me from a Minneapolis supermarket and go to bed with my clothes on, but not to sleep.

I am not a congenitally fearful person, for which you can blame or credit my mother, who never got around to alerting me to any special vulnerabilities that went with being a girl. Only when I got to college did I begin to grasp what rape involves and discover that my custom of exploring strange cities alone, on foot, day or night, looked more reckless to others than eccentric. I had no misgivings about the trailer park in Key West or the motel in Maine, but the trailer's door had a bolt, and both had effective shades and screens. Here, only the stuffiness of the air with the window shut reminds me that I'm really indoors; otherwise I'm pretty much open to anyone's view or to anything that might drift in from the highway, and I wouldn't want to depend on my hosts for help. I think of wearing earplugs to block out the TV sounds from the next room and my sleep mask to cut the light from the Dr Pepper sign on the pop machine in the parking lot. Then I decide it's smarter to keep all senses on ready alert. I sleep and wake up, sleep and wake up again, listen to the cars coming and going, watch the silhouettes move past my window.

Sometime around four in the morning it dawns on me that it's not just that I'm a wimp. Poor women—perhaps especially single ones and even those who are just temporarily living among the poor for whatever reason—really do have more to fear than women who have houses with double locks and alarm systems and husbands or dogs. I must have known this theoretically or at least heard it stated, but now for the first time the lesson takes hold.

So this is the home from which I go forth on Monday to begin my life as a Wal-Martian. After the rigors of orientation, I am expecting a highly structured welcome, perhaps a ceremonial donning of my bright blue Wal-Mart vest and a forty-five-minute training on the operation of the vending machines in the break room. But when I arrive in the morning for the ten-to-six shift, no one seems to be expecting me. I'm in "soft-lines," which has a wonderful, sinuous sound to it, but I have no idea what it means. Someone in personnel tells me I'm in ladies' wear (a division of softlines, I learn) and sends me to the counter next to the fitting rooms, where I am passed around from one person to the next—finally ending up with Ellie, whose lack of a vest signals that she is management. She sets me to work "zoning" the Bobbie Brooks knit summer dresses, a task that could serve as an IQ test for the severely cognitively challenged. First the dresses must be grouped by color—olive, peach, or lavender, in this case—then by decorative pattern—the leafy design on the bodice, the single flower, or the grouped flowers—and within each pattern by size. When I am finished, though hardly exhausted by the effort, I meet Melissa, who is, with only a couple of weeks on the job, pretty much my equivalent. She asks me to help her consolidate the Kathie Lee knit dresses so the Kathie Lee silky ones can take their place at the "image," the high-traffic corner area. I learn, in a couple of hours of scattered exchanges, that Melissa was a waitress before this job, that her husband works in construction and her children are grown. There have been some disorganized patches in her life—an out-of-wedlock child, a problem with alcohol and drugs—but that's all over now that she has given her life to Christ.

Our job, it emerges in fragments throughout the day, is to keep ladies' wear "shoppable." Sure, we help customers (who are increasingly called "guests" here as well), if they want any help. At first I go around practicing the "aggressive hospitality" demanded by our training videos: as soon as anyone comes within ten feet of a sales associate, that associate is supposed to smile warmly and offer assistance. But I never see a more experienced associate do this—first, because the customers are often annoyed to have their shopping dazes interrupted and, second, because we have far more pressing things to do. In ladies' wear, the big task, which has no real equivalent in, say, housewares or lawn and garden, is to put away the "returns"— clothes that have been tried on and rejected or, more rarely, purchased and then returned to the store. There are also the many items that have been scattered by customers, dropped on the floor, removed from their hangers and strewn over the racks, or secreted in locations far from their natural homes. Each of these items, too, must be returned to its precise place, matched by color, pattern, price, and size. Any leftover time is to be devoted to zoning. When I relate this to Caroline on the phone, she commiserates, "Ugh, a no-brainer."

But no job is as easy as it looks to the uninitiated. I have to put clothes away—the question is, Where? Much of my first few days is devoted to trying to memorize the layout of ladies' wear, one thousand (two thousand?) square feet of space bordered by men's wear, children's wear, greeting cards, and underwear. Standing at the fitting rooms and facing toward the main store entrance, we are looking directly at the tentlike, utilitarian plus sizes, also known as "woman" sizes. These are flanked on the left by our dressiest and costliest line (going up to $29 and change), the all-polyester Kathie Lee collection, suitable for dates and subprofessional levels of office work. Moving clockwise, we encounter the determinedly sexless Russ and Bobbie Brooks lines, seemingly aimed at pudgy fourth-grade teachers with important barbecues to attend. Then, after the sturdy White Stag, come the breezy, revealing Faded Glory, No Boundaries, and Jordache collections, designed for the younger and thinner crowd. Tucked throughout are nests of the lesser brands, such as Athletic Works, Basic Equipment, and the whimsical Looney Tunes, Pooh, and Mickey lines, generally decorated with images of their eponymous characters. Within each brand-name area, there are of course dozens of items, even dozens of each *kind* of item. This summer, for example, pants may be capri, classic, carpenter, clam-digger, boot, or flood, depending on their length and cut, and I'm probably leaving a few categories out. So my characteristic stance is one of rotating slowly on one foot, eyes wide, garment in hand, asking myself, "Where have I seen the $9.96 Athletic Works knit overalls?" or similar query. Inevitably there are mystery items requiring extra time and inquiry: clothes that have wandered over from girls' or men's, clearanced items whose tags haven't been changed to reflect their new prices, the occasional one-of-a-kind.

Then, when I have the layout memorized, it suddenly changes. On my third morning I find, after a few futile searches, that the Russ shirt-and-short combinations have edged Kathie Lee out of her image. When I groaningly accuse Ellie of trying to trick me into thinking I'm getting Alzheimer's, she's genuinely apologetic, explaining that the average customer shops the store three times a week, so you need to have the element of surprise. Besides, the layout is about the only thing she *can* control, since the clothes and at least the starting prices are all determined by the home office in Arkansas. So as fast as I can memorize, she furiously rearranges.

My first response to the work is disappointment and a kind of sexist contempt. I could have been in plumbing, mastering the vocabulary of valves, dangling tools from my belt, joshing around with Steve and Walt, and instead the mission of the moment is to return a pink bikini top to its place on the Bermuda swimwear rack. Nothing is heavy or, as far as I can see, very urgent. No one will go hungry or die or be hurt if I screw up; in fact, how would anyone ever know if I screwed up, given the customers' constant depredations? I feel oppressed, too, by the mandatory gentility of Wal-Mart culture. This is ladies' and we are all "ladies" here, forbidden, by storewide rule, to raise our voices or cuss. Give me a few weeks of this and I'll femme out entirely, my stride will be reduced to a mince, I'll start tucking my head down to one side.

My job is not, however, as genteel as it at first appears, thanks to the sheer volume of clothing in motion. At Wal-Mart, as opposed to say Lord & Taylor, customers shop with supermarket-style shopping carts, which they can fill to the brim before proceeding to the fitting room. There the rejected items, which are about 90 percent of try-ons, are folded and put on hangers by whoever is staffing the fitting room, then placed in fresh shopping carts for Melissa and me. So this is how we measure our workload—in carts. When I get in, Melissa, whose shift begins earlier than mine, will tell me how things have been going—"Can you believe, eight carts this morning!"—and how many carts are awaiting me. At first a cart takes me an average of forty-five minutes and there may still be three or four mystery items left at the bottom. I get this down to half an hour, and still the carts keep coming.

Most of the time, the work requires minimal human inter-action, of either the collegial or the supervisory sort, largely because it's so self-defining. I arrive at the start of a shift or the end of a break, assess the damage wrought by the guests in my absence, count the full carts that await me, and plunge in. I could be a deaf-mute as far as most of this goes, and despite all the orientation directives to smile and exude personal warmth, autism might be a definite advantage. Sometimes, if things are slow, Melissa and I will invent a task we can do together—zoning swimsuits, for example, a nightmarish tangle of straps—and giggle, she in her Christian way, me from a more feminist perspective, about the useless little see-through wraps meant to accompany the more revealing among them. Or sometimes Ellie will give me something special to do, like putting all the Basic Equipment T-shirts on hangers, because things on hang-ers sell faster, and then arranging them neatly on racks. I like Ellie. Gray-faced and fiftyish, she must be the apotheosis of "servant leadership" or, in more secular terms, the vaunted "feminine" style of management. She says "please" and "thank you"; she doesn't order, she asks. Not so, though, with young Howard—*assistant manager* Howard, as he is uniformly called—who rules over all of softlines, including infants', children's, men's, accessories, and underwear. On my first day, I am called off the floor to an associates' meeting, where he spends ten minutes taking attendance, fixing each of us with his unnerving Tom Cruise–style smile, in which the brows come together as the corners of the mouth turn up, then reveals (where have I heard this before?) his "pet peeve": associates standing around talking to one another, which is, of course, a prime example of time theft.

A few days into my career at Wal-Mart, I return home to the Clearview to find the door to my room open and the motel owner waiting outside. There's been a "problem"—the sewage has backed up and is all over the floor, though fortunately my suitcase is OK. I am to move into Room 127, which will be better because it has a screen. But the screen turns out to be in tatters, not even fastened at the bottom, just flapping uselessly in the breeze. I ask for a real screen, and he tells me he doesn't have any that fit. I ask for a fan and he doesn't have any that work. I ask why—I mean, this is supposedly a working motel— and he rolls his eyes, apparently indicating my fellow residents: "I could tell you stories . . ."

So I lug my possessions down to 127 and start trying to reconstruct my little domestic life. Since I don't have a kitchen, I have what I call my food bag, a supermarket bag containing my tea bags, a few pieces of fruit, various condiment packets salvaged from fast-food places, and a half dozen string cheeses, which their labels say are supposed to be refrigerated but I figure are safe in their plastic wraps. I have my laptop computer, the essential link to my normal profession, and it has become a matter of increasing concern. I figure it's probably the costliest portable item in the entire Clearview Inn, so I hesitate to leave it in my room for the nine or so hours while I'm away at work.

During the first couple of days at Wal-Mart, the weather was cool and I kept it in the trunk of my car. But now, with the temperature rising to the nineties at midday, I worry that it'll cook in the trunk. More to the point at the moment is the state of my clothing, most of which is now residing in the other brown paper bag, the one that serves as a hamper. My khakis have a day or two left in them and two clean T-shirts remain until the next trip to a Laundromat, but a question has been raised about the T-shirts. That afternoon Alyssa, one of my co-orientees, now in sporting goods, had come by ladies' to inquire about a polo shirt that had been clearanced at $7. Was there any chance it might fall still further? Of course I had no idea—Ellie decides about clearancing—but why was Alyssa so fixated on this particular shirt? Because one of the rules is that our shirts have to have collars, so they have to be polos, not tees. Somehow I'd missed this during orientation, and now I'm wondering how long I have before my stark-naked neck catches Howard's attention. At $7 an hour, a $7 shirt is just not going to make it to my shopping list.

Now it's after seven and time to resume my daily routine at the evening food-gathering phase. The town of Clearview presents only two low-priced options (there are no high-priced options) to its kitchenless residents—a Chinese all-you-can-eat buffet or Kentucky Fried Chicken—each with its own entertainment possibilities. If I eat out at the buffet I can watch the large Mexican families or the even larger, in total body mass terms, families of Minnesota Anglos. If I eat KFC in my room, I can watch TV on one of the half dozen available channels. The latter option seems somehow less lonely, especially if I can find one of my favorite programs—*Titus* or *Third Rock from the Sun*. Eating is tricky without a table. I put the food on the chest of drawers and place a plastic supermarket bag over my lap, since spills are hard to avoid when you eat on a slant and spills mean time and money at the Laundromat. Tonight I find the new sensation, *Survivor,* on CBS, where "real people" are struggling to light a fire on their desert island. Who are these nutcases who would volunteer for an artificially daunting situation in order to entertain millions of strangers with their half-assed efforts to survive? Then I remember where I am and why I am here.

Dinner over, I put the remains in the plastic bag that served as a tablecloth and tie it up tightly to discourage the flies that have free access to my essentially screenless abode. I do my evening things—writing in my journal and reading a novel— then turn out the lights and sit for a while by the open door for some air. The two African American men who live in the room next door have theirs open too, and since it's sometimes open in the daytime as well, I've noticed that their room, like mine, has only one bed. This is no gay tryst, though, because they seem to take turns in the bed, one sleeping in the room and the other one napping in their van outside. I shut the door, put the window down, and undress in the dark so I can't be seen through the window. I still haven't found out much about my fellow Clearview dwellers—it's bad enough being a woman alone, especially a woman rich enough to have a bed of her own, without being nosy on top of that. As far as I can tell, the place isn't a nest of drug dealers and prostitutes; these are just working people who don't have the capital to rent a normal apartment. Even the teenagers who worried me at first seem to have mother figures attached to them, probably single mothers I hadn't seen before because they were at work.

Finally I lie down and breathe against the weight of unmoving air on my chest. I wake up a few hours later to hear a sound not generated by anyone's TV: a woman's clear alto singing two lines of the world's saddest song, lyrics indecipherable, to the accompaniment of trucks on the highway.

Morning begins with a trip, by car, to the Holiday gas station's convenience store, where I buy a pop container full of ice and a packet of two hard-boiled eggs. The ice, a commodity unavailable at the motel, is for iced tea, which I brew by letting tea bags soak in a plastic cup of water overnight. After breakfast I tidy up my room, making the bed, wiping the sink with a wad of toilet paper, and taking the garbage out to the Dumpster. True, the owner's wife (or maybe she's the co-owner) goes around from room to room every morning with a cleaning cart, but her efforts show signs of deep depression or possibly attention deficit disorder. Usually she remembers to replace the thin little towels, which, even when clean, contain embedded hairs and smell like cooking grease, but there's nothing else, except maybe an abandoned rag or bottle of air freshener, to suggest that she's been through on her rounds. I picture an ad for a "traditional-minded, hardworking wife," a wedding in her natal village, then—plop—she's in Clearview, Minnesota, with an Indian American husband who may not even speak her language, thousands of miles from family, a temple, a sari shop.[6] So I clean up myself, then do my hair with enough bobby pins to last through the shift, and head off for work. The idea is to make myself look like someone who's spent the night in a

[6] I thank Sona Pai, an Indian American graduate student in literary nonfiction at the University of Oregon, for giving me a glimpse into the Indian American motel-operating community and the lives of immigrant brides.

regular home with kitchen and washer and dryer, not like someone who's borderline homeless.

The other point of my domestic rituals and arrangements is to get through the time when I can't be at work, when it would look weird to be hanging around in the Wal-Mart parking lot or break room. Because home life is more stressful than I have consciously acknowledged, and I would be dreading my upcoming day off if I weren't confident of spending it on the move to better quarters at the Hopkins Park Plaza. Little nervous symptoms have arisen. Sometimes I get a tummy ache after breakfast, which makes lunch dicey, and there's no way to get through the shift without at least one major refueling. More disturbing is the new habit of plucking away at my shirt or my khakis with whichever hand can be freed up for the task. I have to stop this. My maternal grandmother, who still lives on, in a fashion, at the age of a hundred and one, was a perfect model of stoicism, but she used to pick at her face and her wrist, creating dark red circular sores, and claimed not to know she was doing it. Maybe it's an inheritable twitch and I will soon be moving on from fabric to flesh.

I arrive at work full of bounce, pausing at the fitting room to jolly up the lady on duty—usually the bossy, self-satisfied Rhoda—because the fitting room lady bears the same kind of relation to me as a cook to a server: she can screw me up if she wants, giving me carts contaminated with foreign, nonladies' items and items not properly folded or hangered. "Here I am," I announce grandiosely, spreading out my arms. "The day can begin!" For this I get a wrinkled nose from Rhoda and a one-sided grin from Lynne, the gaunt blonde who's working bras. I search out Ellie, whom I find shooting out new labels from the pricing gun, and ask if there's anything special I need to be doing. No, just whatever needs to be done. Next I find Melissa to get a report on the cartage so far. Today she seems embarrassed when she sees me: "I probably shouldn't have done this and you're going to think it's really silly . . ." but she's brought me a sandwich for lunch. This is because I'd told her I was living in a motel almost entirely on fast food, and she felt sorry for me. Now *I'm* embarrassed, and beyond that overwhelmed to discover a covert stream of generosity running counter to the dominant corporate miserliness. Melissa probably wouldn't think of herself as poor, but I know she calculates in very small units of currency, twice reminding me, for example, that you can get sixty-eight cents off the specials at the Radio Grill every Tuesday, so a sandwich is something to consider. I set off with my cart, muttering contentedly, "Bobbie Brooks turquoise elastic-waist shorts" and "Faded Glory V-neck red tank top."

Then, in my second week, two things change. My shift changes from 10:00–6:00 to 2:00–11:00, the so-called closing shift, although the store remains open 24/7. No one tells me this; I find it out by studying the schedules that are posted, under glass, on the wall outside the break room. Now I have nine hours instead of eight, and although one of them is an unpaid dinner hour, I have a net half an hour a day more on my feet. My two fifteen-minute breaks, which seemed almost superfluous on the 10:00–6:00 shift, now become a matter of urgent calculation. Do I take both before dinner, which is usually about 7:30, leaving an unbroken two-and-a-half-hour stretch when I'm weariest, between 8:30 and 11:00? Or do I try to go two and a half hours without a break in the afternoon, followed by a nearly three-hour marathon before I can get away for dinner? Then there's the question of how to make the best use of a fifteen-minute break when you have three or more urgent, simultaneous needs—to pee, to drink something, to get outside the neon and into the natural light, and most of all, to sit down. I save about a minute by engaging in a little time theft and stopping at the rest room before I punch out for the break (and, yes, we have to punch out even for breaks, so there's no padding them with a few stolen minutes). From the time clock it's a seventy-five-second walk to the store exit; if I stop at the Radio Grill, I could end up wasting a full four minutes waiting in line, not to mention the fifty-nine cents for a small-sized iced tea. So if I treat myself to an outing in the tiny fenced-off area beside the store, the only place where employees are allowed to smoke, I get about nine minutes off my feet.

The other thing that happens is that the post–Memorial Day weekend lull definitely comes to an end. Now there are always a dozen or more shoppers rooting around in ladies', reinforced in the evening by a wave of multigenerational gangs—Grandma, Mom, a baby in the shopping cart, and a gaggle of sullen children in tow. New tasks arise, such as bunching up the carts left behind by customers and steering them to their place in the front of the store every half hour or so. Now I am picking up not only dropped clothes but all the odd items customers carry off from foreign departments and decide to leave with us in ladies'—pillows, upholstery hooks, Pokémon cards, earrings, sunglasses, stuffed animals, even a package of cinnamon buns. And always there are the returns, augmented now by the huge volume of items that have been tossed on the floor or carried fecklessly to inappropriate sites. Sometimes I am lucky to achieve a steady state between replacing the returns and picking up items strewn on the racks and the floor. If I pick up misplaced items as quickly as I replace the returns, my cart never empties and things back up dangerously at the fitting room, where Rhoda or her nighttime replacement is likely to hiss: "You've got three carts waiting, Barb. What's the *problem*?" Think Sisyphus here or the sorcerer's apprentice.

Still, for the first half of my shift, I am the very picture of good-natured helpfulness, fascinated by the multiethnic array of our shoppers—Middle Eastern, Asian, African American, Russian, former Yugoslavian, old-fashioned Minnesota white—and calmly accepting of the second law of thermodynamics, the one that says entropy always wins. Amazingly, I get praised by Isabelle, the thin little seventyish lady who seems to be Ellie's adjutant: I am doing "wonderfully," she tells me, and—even better—am "great to work with." I prance from rack to rack, I preen. But then, somewhere around 6:00 or 7:00, when the desire to sit down becomes a serious craving, a Dr. Jekyll/Mr. Hyde transformation sets in. I cannot ignore the fact that it's the customers' sloppiness and idle whims that make me bend and crouch and run. They are the shoppers, I am the antishopper, whose goal is to make it look as if they'd never been in the store. At this point, "aggressive hospitality" gives way to aggressive hostility. Their carts bang into mine, their children run amok. Once I stand and watch helplessly while some rug rat pulls everything he can reach off the racks, and the thought that abortion is wasted on the unborn must show on my face, because his mother finally tells him to stop.

I even start hating the customers for extraneous reasons, such as, in the case of the native Caucasians, their size. I don't mean just bellies and butts, but huge bulges in completely exotic locations, like the backs of the neck and the knees. This summer, Wendy's, where I often buy lunch, has introduced the verb *biggiesize,* as in "Would you like to biggiesize that combo?" meaning double the fries and pop, and something like biggiesizing seems to have happened to the female guest population. All right, everyone knows that midwesterners, and especially those in the lower middle class, are tragically burdened by the residues of decades of potato chips and French toast sticks, and I probably shouldn't even bring this up. In my early-shift, Dr. Jekyll form, I feel sorry for the obese, who must choose from among our hideous woman-size offerings, our drawstring shorts, and huge horizontally striped tees, which are obviously designed to mock them. But compassion fades as the shift wears on. Those of us who work in ladies' are for obvious reasons a pretty lean lot—probably, by Minnesota standards, candidates for emergency IV nutritional supplementation—and we live with the fear of being crushed by some wide-body as she hurtles through the narrow passage from Faded Glory to woman size, lost in fantasies involving svelte Kathie Lee sheaths.

It's the clothes I relate to, though, not the customers. And now a funny thing happens to me here on my new shift: I start thinking they're mine, not mine to take home and wear, because I have no such designs on them, just mine to organize and rule over. Same with ladies' wear as a whole. After 6:00, when Melissa and Ellie go home, and especially after 9:00, when Isabelle leaves, I start to *own* the place. Out of the way, Sam, this is Bar-Mart now. I patrol the perimeter with my cart, darting in to pick up misplaced and fallen items, making everything look spiffy from the outside. I don't fondle the clothes, the way customers do; I slap them into place, commanding them to hang straight, at attention, or lie subdued on the shelves in perfect order. In this frame of mind, the last thing I want to see is a customer riffling around, disturbing the place.

In fact, I hate the idea of things being sold—uprooted from their natural homes, whisked off to some closet that's in God-knows-what state of disorder. I want ladies' wear sealed off in a plastic bubble and trucked away to some place of safety, some museum of retail history.

One night I come back bone-tired from my last break and am distressed to find a new person, an Asian American or possibly Hispanic woman who can't be more than four and a half feet tall, folding T-shirts in the White Stag area, *my* White Stag area. It's already been a vexing evening. Earlier, when I'd returned from dinner, the evening fitting room lady upbraided me for being late—which I actually wasn't—and said that if Howard knew, he probably wouldn't yell at me this time because I'm still pretty new, but if it happened again . . . And I'd snapped back that I could care less if Howard yelled at me, which is a difficult sentiment to fully convey without access to the forbidden four-letter words. So I'm a little wary with this intruder in White Stag and, sure enough, after our minimal introductions, she turns on me.

"Did you put anything away here today?" she demands.

"Well, yes, sure." In fact I've put something away everywhere today, as I do on every other day.

"Because this is not in the right place. See the fabric—it's different," and she thrusts the errant item up toward my chest.

True, I can see that this olive-green shirt is slightly ribbed while the others are smooth. "You've *got* to put them in their right places," she continues. "Are you checking the UPC numbers?"

Of course I am not checking the ten or more digit UPC numbers, which lie just under the bar codes—nobody does. What does she think this is, the National Academy of Sciences?

I'm not sure what kind of deference, if any, is due here: Is she my supervisor now? Or are we involved in some kind of test to see who will dominate the 9:00–11:00 time period? But I don't care, she's pissing me off, messing with my stuff. So I say, only without the numerals or the forbidden curse word, that (1) plenty of other people work here during the day, not to mention all the customers coming through, so why is she blaming me? (2) it's after 10:00 and I've got another cart full of returns to go, and wouldn't it make more sense if we both worked on the carts, instead of zoning the goddamn T-shirts?

To which she responds huffily, "I don't *do* returns. My job is to *fold*."

A few minutes later I see why she doesn't do returns—she can't reach the racks. In fact, she has to use a ladder even to get to the higher shelves. And you know what I feel when I see the poor little mite pushing that ladder around? A surge of evil mirth. I peer around from where I am working in Jordache, hoping to see her go splat.

I leave that night shaken by my response to the intruder. If she's a supervisor, I could be written up for what I said, but even worse is what I thought. Am I turning mean here, and is that a normal response to the end of a nine-hour shift? There was another outbreak of mental wickedness that night. I'd gone back to the counter by the fitting room to pick up the next cart full of returns and found the guy who answers the phone at the counter at night, a pensive young fellow in a wheelchair, staring into space, looking even sadder than usual. And my uncensored thought was, At least you get to sit down.

This is not me, at least not any version of me I'd like to spend much time with, just as my tiny coworker is probably not usually a bitch. She's someone who works all night and naps during the day when her baby does, I find out later, along with the information that she's not anyone's supervisor and is in fact subject to constant criticism by Isabelle when the two overlap. What I have to face is that "Barb," the name on my ID tag, is not exactly the same person as Barbara. "Barb" is what I was called as a child, and still am by my siblings, and I sense that at some level I'm regressing. Take away the career and the higher education, and maybe what you're left with is this original Barb, the one who might have ended up working at Wal-Mart for real if her father hadn't managed to climb out of the mines. So it's interesting, and more than a little disturbing, to see how Barb turned out—that she's meaner and slyer than I am, more cherishing of grudges, and not quite as smart as I'd hoped.

ON THE DAY OF MY MOVE TO THE HOPKINS PARK PLAZA, I WAKE UP savoring the thought of the perishables I'm going to stock my refrigerator with: mayonnaise, mustard, chicken breasts. But when I get there Hildy is gone and the woman in the towering black beehive who has taken her place says I didn't understand, the room won't be available until *next* week and I should call first to be sure. Had I really been so befogged by wishful thinking that I'd "misunderstood" what had seemed to be a fairly detailed arrangement (bring your money down at nine on Saturday, you can move in at four, etc.)? Or had someone else just beat me to it? Never mind, I've been clearheaded enough to know all along that the Park Plaza apartment with kitchenette, at $179 a week, was not a long-term option on Wal-Mart's $7 an hour. My plan had been to add a weekend job, which I have been tentatively offered at a Rainbow supermarket near the apartment where I originally stayed, at close to $8 an hour.

Between the two jobs, I would be making about $320 a week after taxes, so that the $179 in rent would have amounted to about 55 percent of my income, which is beginning to look "affordable."[7] But Rainbow also falls through; they decide they want me to work part-time five days a week, not just on weekends. Furthermore, I have no control at the moment over what my days off will be. Howard has scheduled me to have Friday off one week, Tuesday and Wednesday the next, and I would have to do some serious sucking up to arrive at a more stable and congenial schedule.

Ergo, I either need to find a husband, like Melissa, or a second job, like some of my other coworkers. In the long run everything will work out if I devote my mornings to job hunting, while holding out for a Park Plaza opening or, better yet, a legitimate apartment at $400 a month or $100 a week. But to paraphrase Keynes: in the long run, we'll all be broke, at least those of us who work for low wages and live in exorbitantly overpriced motels. I call the YWCA to see whether they have any rooms, and they refer me to a place called Budget Lodging,

[7] Actually, rents usually have to be less than 30 percent of one's income to be considered "affordable." Housing analyst Peter Dreier reports that 59 percent of poor renters, amounting to a total of 4.4 million households, spend more than 50 percent of their income on shelter ("Why America's Workers Can't Pay the Rent," *Dissent,* Summer 2000, pp. 38–44). A 1996–97 survey of 44,461 households found that 28 percent of parents with incomes less than 200 percent of the poverty level—i.e., less than about $30,000 a year—reported problems paying their rent, mortgage, or utility bills (*Welfare Reform Network News* 1:2 [March 1999], Institute for Women's Policy Research, Washington, D.C.). In the Twin Cities, at the time of my stay, about 46,000 working families were paying more than 50 percent of their income for housing, and, surprisingly, 73 percent of these families were home owners hard-pressed by rising property taxes ("Affordable Housing Problem Hits Moderate-Income Earners," *Minneapolis Star Tribune,* July 12, 2000). ·

which doesn't have any rooms either, although they do have dorm beds for $19 a night. I can have my own locker and there's no "lockout" in the morning—you can hang out in your dorm bed all day if you want. Even with these enticements, I have to admit I'm relieved when the guy at Budget Lodging tells me they're located on the other side of Minneapolis, so I can rule out the dorm on account of the drive and the gas costs, at least as long as I'm working at Wal-Mart. Maybe I should have just dumped Wal-Mart, moved into the dorm, and relaunched my job search from there. But the truth is I'm not ready to leave Wal-Mart yet; it's my connection to the world, my source of identity, my *place*.

The Budget Lodging clerk, who seems to have some familiarity with the housing nightmares of low-wage workers, suggests I keep trying motels. He's sure there must be some that cost less than $240 a week. In the meantime, the Clearview Inn wants an unconscionable $55 for any additional nights there, which means that, for a couple of nights, almost any motel would be preferable. I call Caroline to ask for her insights into the housing situation and—I should have guessed this was coming—she calls back in a few minutes to invite me to move in with her and her family. I say no, I've already had a stint of free lodging and now I have to take my chances with the market like anyone else. But for a moment I get this touched-by-an-angel feeling I'd gotten from Melissa's sandwich: I am not really entirely alone. I start calling around to motels again, now ranging even farther out from the city, into the northern towns, the western towns, St. Paul. But most have no rooms at all, at any price, either now or for the coming weeks—because of the season, I'm told, although it's hard to see why a place like, say, Clearview, Minnesota, would be a destination at any time of the year. Only the Comfort Inn has a room available, at $49.95 a night, so I make a reservation there for a couple of days. The relief I should feel about leaving the Worst Motel in the Country is canceled by an overwhelming sense of defeat.

Could I have done better? The *St. Paul Pioneer Press* of June 13, which I eagerly snatch out of the box in front of Wal-Mart, provides an overdue reality check. "Apartment rents skyrocket," the front-page headline declares; they've leaped 20.5 percent in Minneapolis in the first three months of 2000 alone, an unprecedented increase, according to local real estate experts. Even more pertinent to my condition, the Twin Cities region "is posting one of the lowest vacancy rates in the nation—possibly the lowest." Who knew? My cursory pre-trip research had revealed nothing about a record absence of housing. In fact, I'd come across articles bemoaning the absence of a Twin Cities dot-com industry, and these had led me to believe that the region had been spared the wild real estate inflation afflicting, for example, California's Bay Area. But apparently you don't need dot-com wealth to ruin an area for its low-income residents. The *Pioneer Press* quotes Secretary of HUD Andrew Cuomo ruing the "cruel irony" that prosperity is shrinking the stock of affordable housing nationwide: "The stronger the economy, the stronger the upward pressure on rents." So I'm a victim not of poverty but of prosperity. The rich and the poor, who are generally thought to live in a state of harmonious interdependence—the one providing cheap labor, the other providing low-wage jobs—can no longer coexist.

I check in at the Comfort Inn in the firm expectation that this will be only for a night or two, before something, somewhere, opens up to me. What I cannot know is that this is, in some sense, my moment of final defeat. Game over. End of story—at least if it's a story about attempting to match earnings to rent. In almost three weeks, I've spent over $500 and earned only $42—from Wal-Mart, for orientation night. There's more coming eventually—Wal-Mart, like so many other low-wage employers, holds back your first week's pay—but eventually will be too late.

I never do find an apartment or affordable motel, although I do make one last attempt, seeking help one morning at a charitable agency. I found the place by calling United Way of Minneapolis, which directed me to another agency, which in turn directed me to something called the Community Emergency Assistance Program, located a convenient fifteen-minute drive from Wal-Mart. Inside the office suite housing CEAP, a disturbing scene is unfolding: two rail-thin black men—Somalis, I guess, from their accents and since there are a lot of them in the Twin Cities area—are saying, "Bread? Bread?" and being told, "No bread, no bread." They flutter out and a fiftyish white woman comes in and goes through the same routine, leaving with the smile of supplication still frozen awkwardly on her face. For some reason, though—perhaps because I have an appointment and haven't worn out my welcome yet—I get taken to an inner office where a young woman interviews me absentmindedly. Do I have a car? Yes, I have a car. And a couple of minutes later: "So you don't have a car?" and so forth.

When I tell her I'm working at Wal-Mart and what I earn, she suggests I move into a shelter so I can save up enough money for a first month's rent and deposit, then she sends me to another office where she says I can apply for a housing subsidy and get help finding an apartment. But this other office offers only a photocopied list of affordable apartments, which is updated weekly and is already out of date. Back at the first office, my interviewer asks if I can use some emergency food aid and I explain, once again, that I don't have a refrigerator. She'll find something, she says, and comes back with a box containing a bar of soap, a deodorant, and a bunch of fairly useless food items, from my point of view—lots of candy and cookies and a one-pound can of ham, which, without a refrigerator, I would have to eat all in one sitting.[8] (The next day I take the whole box, untouched, to another agency serving the poor, so I won't appear ungrateful and the food won't be wasted.)

Only when I'm driving away with my sugary loot do I realize the importance of what I've learned in this encounter. At one point toward the end of the interview, the CEAP lady had apologized for forgetting almost everything I said about myself—that I had a car, lived in a motel, etc. She was mixing me up with someone else who worked at Wal-Mart, she explained, someone who had been in just a few days ago. Now, of course I've noticed that many of my coworkers are poor in all the hard-to-miss, stereotypical ways. Crooked yellow teeth are one sign, inadequate footwear is another. My feet hurt after

---

[8] Middle-class people often criticize the poor for their eating habits, but this charitable agency seemed to be promoting a reliance on "empty calories." The complete inventory of the box of free food I received is as follows: 21 ounces of General Mills Honey Nut Chex cereal; 24 ounces of Post Grape-Nuts cereal; 20 ounces of Mississippi Barbecue Sauce; several small plastic bags of candy, including Tootsie Rolls, Smarties fruit snacks, Sweet Tarts, and two bars of Ghirardelli chocolate; one bubble gum; a 13-ounce package of iced sugar cookies; hamburger buns; six 6-ounce Minute Maid juice coolers; one loaf of Vienna bread; Star Wars fruit snacks; one loaf of cinnamon bread; 18 ounces of peanut butter; 18 ounces of jojoba shampoo; 16 ounces of canned ham; one bar of Dial soap; four Kellogg Rice Krispies Treats bars; two Ritz cracker packages; one 5-ounce Swanson canned chicken breast; 2 ounces of a Kool-Aid-like drink mix; two Lady Speed Stick deodorants.

four hours of work, and I wear my comfortable old Reeboks, but a lot of women run around all day in thin-soled moccasins. Hair provides another class cue. Ponytails are common or, for that characteristic Wal-Martian beat-up and hopeless look, straight shoulder-length hair, parted in the middle and kept out of the face by two bobby pins.

But now I know something else. In orientation, we learned that the store's success depends entirely on us, the associates; in fact, our bright blue vests bear the statement "At Wal-Mart, our people make the difference." Underneath those vests, though, there are real-life charity cases, maybe even shelter dwellers.[9]

SO, ANYWAY, BEGINS MY SURREAL EXISTENCE AT THE COMFORT INN. I live in luxury with AC, a door that bolts, a large window protected by an intact screen—just like a tourist or a business traveler. But from there I go out every day to a life that most business travelers would find shabby and dispiriting—lunch at Wendy's, dinner at Sbarro (the Italian-flavored fast-food place), and work at Wal-Mart, where I would be embarrassed to be discovered in my vest, should some member of the Comfort staff happen to wander in. Of course, I expect to leave any day, when the Hopkins Park Plaza opens up. For the time being, though, I revel in the splendor of my accommodations, amazed that they cost $5.05 less, on a daily basis, than what I was paying for that rat hole in Clearview. I stop worrying about my

[9] In 1988, Arkansas state senator Jay Bradford attacked Wal-Mart for paying its employees so little that they had to turn to the state for welfare. He was, however, unable to prove his point by getting the company to open its payroll records (Bob Ortega, *In Sam We Trust: The Untold Story of Sam Walton and Wal-Mart, the World's Most Powerful Retailer* [Times Books, 2000], p. 193).

computer being stolen or cooked, I sleep through the night, the sick little plucking habit loses its grip. I feel like the man in the commercials for the Holiday Inn Express who's so refreshed by his overnight stay that he can perform surgery the next day or instruct people in how to use a parachute. At Wal-Mart, I get better at what I do, much better than I could ever have imagined at the beginning.

The breakthrough comes on a Saturday, one of your heavier shopping days. There are two carts waiting for me when I arrive at two, and tossed items inches deep on major patches of the floor. The place hasn't been shopped, it's been looted. In this situation, all I can do is everything at once—stoop, reach, bend, lift, run from rack to rack with my cart. And then it happens—a magical flow state in which the clothes start putting *themselves* away. Oh, I play a part in this, but not in any conscious way. Instead of thinking, "White Stag navy twill skort," and doggedly searching out similar skorts, all I have to do is form an image of the item in my mind, transpose this image onto the visual field, and move to wherever the image finds its match in the outer world. I don't know how this works. Maybe my mind just gets so busy processing the incoming visual data that it has to bypass the left brain's verbal centers, with their cumbersome instructions: "Proceed to White Stag area in the northwest corner of ladies', try bottom racks near khaki shorts . . ." Or maybe the trick lies in understanding that each item *wants* to be reunited with its sibs and its clan members and that, within each clan, the item *wants* to occupy its proper place in the color/size hierarchy. Once I let the clothes take charge, once I understand that I am only the means of their reunification, they just fly out of the cart to their natural homes.

On the same day, perhaps because the new speediness frees me to think more clearly, I make my peace with the customers and discover the purpose of life, or at least of my life at Wal-Mart. Management may think that the purpose is to sell things, but this is an overly reductionist, narrowly capitalist view. As a matter of fact, I never see anything sold, since sales take place out of my sight, at the cash registers at the front of the store. All I see is customers unfolding carefully folded T-shirts, taking dresses and pants off their hangers, holding them up for a moment's idle inspection, then dropping them somewhere for us associates to pick up. For me, the way out of resentment begins with a clue provided by a poster near the break room, in the back of the store where only associates go: "Your mother doesn't work here," it says. "Please pick up after yourself." I've passed it many times, thinking, "Ha, that's all I do—pick up after people." Then it hits me: most of the people I pick up after are mothers themselves, meaning that what I do at work is what *they* do at home—pick up the toys and the clothes and the spills. So the great thing about shopping, for most of these women, is that here *they* get to behave like brats, ignoring the bawling babies in their carts, tossing things around for someone else to pick up. And it wouldn't be any fun—would it?—unless the clothes were all reasonably orderly to begin with, which is where I come in, constantly re-creating orderliness for the customers to maliciously destroy. It's appalling, but it's in their nature: only pristine and virginal displays truly excite them.

I test this theory out on Isabelle: that our job is to constantly re-create the stage setting in which women can act out. That without us, rates of child abuse would suddenly soar. That we function, in a way, as therapists and should probably be paid accordingly, at $50 to $100 an hour. "You just go on thinking that," she says, shaking her head. But she smiles her canny little smile in a way that makes me think it's not a bad notion.

With competence comes a new impatience: *Why does anybody put up with the wages we're paid?* True, most of my fellow workers are better cushioned than I am; they live with spouses or grown children or they have other jobs in addition to this one. I sit with Lynne in the break room one night and find out this is only a part-time job for her—six hours a day—with the other eight hours spent at a factory for $9 an hour. Doesn't she get awfully tired? Nah, it's what she's always done. The cook at the Radio Grill has two other jobs. You might expect a bit of grumbling, some signs here and there of unrest—graffiti on the hortatory posters in the break room, muffled guffaws during our associate meetings—but I can detect none of that. Maybe this is what you get when you weed out all the rebels with drug tests and personality "surveys"—a uniformly servile and denatured workforce, content to dream of the distant day when they'll be vested in the company's profit-sharing plan. They even join in the "Wal-Mart cheer" when required to do so at meetings, I'm told by the evening fitting room lady, though I am fortunate enough never to witness this final abasement.[10]

But if it's hard to think "out of the box," it may be almost impossible to think out of the Big Box. Wal-Mart, when you're

---

[10] According to Wal-Mart expert Bob Ortega, Sam Walton got the idea for the cheer on a 1975 trip to Japan, "where he was deeply impressed by factory workers doing group calisthenics and company cheers." Ortega describes Walton conducting a cheer: "'Gimme a W!' he'd shout. 'W!' the workers would shout back, and on through the Wal-Mart name. At the hyphen, Walton would shout 'Gimme a squiggly!' and squat and twist his hips at the same time; the workers would squiggle right back" (*In Sam We Trust*, p. 91).

in it, is total—a closed system, a world unto itself. I get a chill when I'm watching TV in the break room one afternoon and see . . . *a commercial for Wal-Mart*. When a Wal-Mart shows up within a television within a Wal-Mart, you have to question the existence of an outer world. Sure, you can drive for five minutes and get somewhere else—to Kmart, that is, or Home Depot, or Target, or Burger King, or Wendy's, or KFC. Wherever you look, there is no alternative to the megascale corporate order, from which every form of local creativity and initiative has been abolished by distant home offices. Even the woods and the meadows have been stripped of disorderly life forms and forced into a uniform made of concrete. What you see—highways, parking lots, stores—is all there is, or all that's left to us here in the reign of globalized, totalized, paved-over, corporatized everything. I like to read the labels to find out where the clothing we sell is made—Indonesia, Mexico, Turkey, the Philippines, South Korea, Sri Lanka, Brazil—but the labels serve only to remind me that none of these places is "exotic" anymore, that they've all been eaten by the great blind profit-making global machine.

The only thing to do is ask: Why do you—why do *we*—work here? Why do you stay? So when Isabelle praises my work a second time (!), I take the opportunity to say I really appreciate her encouragement, but I can't afford to live on $7 an hour, and how does she do it? The answer is that she lives with her grown daughter, who also works, plus the fact that she's worked here two years, during which her pay has shot up to $7.75 an hour. She counsels patience: it could happen to me. Melissa, who has the advantage of a working husband, says, "Well, it's a job." Yes, she made twice as much when she was a waitress but that place closed down and at her age she's never going to be hired at a high-tip place. I recognize the inertia, the unwillingness to start up with the apps and the interviews and the drug tests again. She thinks she should give it a year. *A year?* I tell her I'm wondering whether I should give it another week.

A few days later something happens to make kindly, sweet-natured Melissa mad. She gets banished to bras, which is terra incognita for us—huge banks of shelves bearing barely distinguishable bi-coned objects—for a three-hour stretch. I know how she feels, because I was once sent over to work for a couple of hours in men's wear, where I wandered uselessly through the strange thickets of racks, numbed by the sameness of colors and styles.[11] It's the difference between working and pretending to work. You push your cart a few feet, pause significantly with item in hand, frown at the ambient racks, then push on and repeat the process. "I just don't like wasting their money," Melissa says when she's allowed back. "I mean they're *paying* me and I just wasn't accomplishing anything over there." To me, this anger seems badly mis-aimed. What does she think, that the Walton family is living in some hidden room in the back of the store, in the utmost frugality, and likely to be ruined by $21 worth of wasted labor? I'm starting in on that theme when she suddenly dives behind the rack that separates the place where we're standing, in the Jordache/No Boundaries section, from the Faded Glory region. Worried that I may have offended her somehow, I follow right behind. *"Howard,"* she whispers. "Didn't you see him come by? We're not allowed to talk to each other, you know."

[11] "During your career with Wal-Mart, you may be cross-trained in other departments in your facility. This will challenge you in new areas, and help you be a well-rounded Associate" ("Wal-Mart Associate Handbook," p. 18).

"The point is our time is so cheap they don't care if we waste it," I continue, aware even as I speak that this isn't true, otherwise why would they be constantly monitoring us for "time theft"? But I sputter on: "That's what's so insulting." Of course, in this outburst of militance I am completely not noticing the context—two women of mature years, two very hardworking women, as it happens, dodging behind a clothing rack to avoid a twenty-six-year-old management twerp. That's not even worth commenting on.

Alyssa is another target for my crusade. When she returns to check yet again on that $7 polo, she finds a stain on it. What could she get off for that? I think 10 percent, and if you add in the 10 percent employee discount, we'd be down to $5.60. I'm trying to negotiate a 20 percent price reduction with the fitting room lady when—rotten luck!—Howard shows up and announces that there are no reductions and no employee discounts on clearanced items. Those are the rules. Alyssa looks crushed, and I tell her, when Howard's out of sight, that there's something wrong when you're not paid enough to buy a Wal-Mart shirt, a *clearanced* Wal-Mart shirt with a stain on it. "I hear you," she says, and admits Wal-Mart isn't working for her either, if the goal is to make a living.

Then I get a little reckless. When an associate meeting is announced over the loudspeaker that afternoon, I decide to go, although most of my coworkers stay put. I don't understand the purpose of these meetings, which occur every three days or so and consist largely of attendance taking, unless it's Howard's way of showing us that there's only one of him compared to so many of us. I'm just happy to have a few minutes to sit down or, in this case, perch on some fertilizer bags since we're meeting in lawn and garden today, and chat with whoever shows up, today a gal from the optical department. She's better coifed and made up than most of us female associates—forced to take the job because of a recent divorce, she tells me, and sorry now that she's found out how crummy the health insurance is. There follows a long story about preexisting conditions and deductibles and her COBRA running out. I listen vacantly because, like most of the other people in my orientation group, I hadn't opted for the health insurance—the employee contribution seemed too high. "You know what we need here?" I finally respond. "We need a union." There it is, the word is out. Maybe if I hadn't been feeling so footsore I wouldn't have said it, and I probably wouldn't have said it either if we were allowed to say "hell" and "damn" now and then or, better yet, "shit." But no one has outright banned the word *union* and right now it's the most potent couple of syllables at hand. "We need *something,*" she responds.

After that, there's nothing to stop me. I'm on a mission now: *Raise the questions! Plant the seeds!* Breaks finally have a purpose beyond getting off my feet. There are hundreds of workers here—I never do find out how many—and sooner or later I'll meet them all. I reject the break room for this purpose because the TV inhibits conversation, and for all I know that's what it's supposed to do. Better to go outdoors to the fenced-in smoking area in front of the store. Smokers, in smoke-free America, are more likely to be rebels; at least that was true at The Maids, where the nonsmokers waited silently in the office for work to begin, while the smokers out on the sidewalk would be having a raucous old time. Besides, you can always start the ball rolling by asking for a light, which I have to do anyway when the wind is up. The next question is, "What department are you in?" followed by, "How long have you worked here?"—

from which it's an obvious segue to the business at hand. Almost everyone is eager to talk, and I soon become a walking repository of complaints. No one gets paid overtime at Wal-Mart, I'm told, though there's often pressure to work it.[12] Many feel the health insurance isn't worth paying for. There's a lot of frustration over schedules, especially in the case of the evangelical lady who can never get Sunday morning off, no matter how much she pleads. And always there are the gripes about managers: the one who is known for sending new hires home in tears, the one who takes a ruler and knocks everything off what he regards as a messy shelf, so you have to pick it up off the floor and start over.

Sometimes, I discover, my favorite subject, which is the abysmal rate of pay, seems to be a painful one. Stan, for example, a twenty-something fellow with wildly misaligned teeth, is so eager to talk that he fairly pounces on the seat next to mine on a bench in the smoking area. But when the subject

---

[12] Wal-Mart employees have sued the retail chain for unpaid overtime in four states—West Virginia, New Mexico, Oregon, and Colorado. The plaintiffs allege that they were pressured to work overtime and that the company then erased the overtime hours from their time records. Two of the West Virginia plaintiffs, who had been promoted to management positions before leaving Wal-Mart, said they had participated in altering time records to conceal overtime work. Instead of paying time and a half for overtime work, the company would reward workers with "desired schedule changes, promotions and other benefits," while workers who refused the unpaid overtime were "threatened with write-ups, demotions, reduced work schedules or docked pay" (Lawrence Messina, "Former Wal-Mart Workers File Overtime Suit in Harrison County," *Charleston Gazette,* January 24, 1999). In New Mexico, a suit by 110 Wal-Mart employees was settled in 1998 when the company agreed to pay for the overtime ("Wal-Mart Agrees to Resolve Pay Dispute," *Albuquerque Journal,* July 16, 1998). In an e-mail to me, Wal-Mart spokesman William Wertz stated that "it is Wal-Mart's policy to compensate its employees fairly for their work and to comply fully with all federal and state wage and hour requirements."

arrives at wages, his face falls. The idea, see, was that he would go to school (he names a two-year technical school) while he worked, but the work cut into studying too much, so he had to drop out and now . . . He stares at the butt-strewed ground, perhaps seeing an eternity in appliances unfold before him. I suggest that what we need is a union, but from the look on his face I might as well have said gumballs or Prozac. Yeah, maybe he'll go over and apply at Media One, where a friend works and the wages are higher . . . Try school again, umm . . .

At the other extreme, there are people like Marlene. I am sitting out there talking to a doll-like blonde whom I had taken for a high school student but who, it turns out, has been working full-time since November and is fretting over whether she can afford to buy a car. Marlene comes out for her break, lights a cigarette, and emphatically seconds my opinion of Wal-Mart wages. "They talk about having spirit," she says, referring to management, "but they don't give us any reason to have any spirit." In her view, Wal-Mart would rather just keep hiring new people than treating the ones it has decently. You can see for yourself there's a dozen new people coming in for orientation every day—which is true. Wal-Mart's appetite for human flesh is insatiable; we've even been urged to recruit any Kmart employees we may happen to know. They don't care that they've trained you or anything, Marlene goes on, they can always get someone else if you complain. Emboldened by her vehemence, I risk the red-hot word again. "I know this goes against the whole Wal-Mart philosophy, but we could use a union here." She grins, so I push on: "It's not just about money, it's about dignity." She nods fiercely, lighting a second cigarette from her first. *Put that woman on the organizing committee at once,* I direct my imaginary coconspirators as I leave.

All right, I'm not a union organizer anymore than I'm Wal-Mart "management material," as Isabelle has hinted. In fact, I don't share the belief, held by many union staffers, that unionization would be a panacea. Sure, almost any old union would boost wages and straighten out some backbones here, but I know that even the most energetic and democratic unions bear careful watching by their members. The truth, which I can't avoid acknowledging when I'm in those vast, desertlike stretches between afternoon breaks, is that I'm just amusing myself, and in what seems like a pretty harmless way. Someone has to puncture the prevailing fiction that we're a "family" here, we "associates" and our "servant leaders," held together solely by our commitment to the "guests." After all, you'd need a lot stronger word than *dysfunctional* to describe a family where a few people get to eat at the table while the rest—the "associates" and all the dark-skinned seamstresses and factory workers worldwide who make the things we sell—lick up the drippings from the floor: *psychotic* would be closer to the mark.[13] And someone has to flush out the mysterious "we" lurking in the "our" in the "Our people make the difference" statement we wear on our backs. It might as well be me because I have nothing to lose, less than nothing, in fact. For each day that I fail to find cheaper quarters, which is every day now, I am spending $49.95 for the privilege of putting clothes away at Wal-Mart.

[13] In 1996, the National Labor Committee Education Fund in Support of Worker and Human Rights in Central America revealed that some Kathie Lee clothes were being sewn by children as young as twelve in a sweatshop in Honduras. TV personality Kathie Lee Gifford, the owner of the Kathie Lee line, tearfully denied the charges on the air but later promised to give up her dependence on sweatshops.

At this rate, I'll have burned through the rest of the $1,200 I've allotted for my life in Minneapolis in less than a week.

I could use some amusement. I have been discovering a great truth about low-wage work and probably a lot of medium-wage work, too—that nothing happens, or rather the same thing always happens, which amounts, day after day, to nothing. This law doesn't apply so strictly to the service jobs I've held so far. In waitressing, you always have new customers to study; even housecleaning offers the day's parade of houses to explore. But here—well, you know what I do and how it gets undone and how I just start all over and do it again. How did I think I was going to survive in a factory, where each *minute* is identical to the next one, and not just each day? There will be no crises here, except perhaps in the pre-Christmas rush. There will be no "Code M," meaning "hostage situation," and probably no Code F or T (I'm guessing on these letters, which I didn't write down during my note taking at orientation and which may be a company secret anyway), meaning fire or tornado—no opportunities for courage or extraordinary achievement or sudden evacuations of the store. Those breaking-news moments when a disgruntled former employee shoots up the place or a bunch of people get crushed in an avalanche of piled-up stock are one-in-a-million events. What my life holds is carts—full ones, then empty ones, then full ones again.

You could get old pretty fast here. In fact, time does funny things when there are no little surprises to mark it off into memorable chunks, and I sense that I'm already several years older than I was when I started. In the one full-length mirror in ladies' wear, a medium-tall figure is hunched over a cart, her face pinched in absurd concentration—surely not me. How long before I'm as gray as Ellie, as cranky as Rhoda, as shriveled as Isabelle? When even a high-sodium fast-food diet can't keep me from needing to pee every hour, and my feet are putting some podiatrist's kid through college? Yes, I know that any day now I'm going to return to the variety and drama of my real, Barbara Ehrenreich life. But this fact sustains me only in the way that, say, the prospect of heaven cheers a terminally ill person: it's nice to know, but it isn't much help from moment to moment. What you don't necessarily realize when you start selling your time by the hour is that what you're actually selling is your *life*.

Then something happens, not to me and not at Wal-Mart but with dazzling implications nonetheless. It's a banner headline in the *Star Tribune:* 1,450 hotel workers, members of the Hotel Employees and Restaurant Employees Union, strike nine local hotels. A business writer in the *Pioneer Press,* commenting on this plus a Teamsters' strike at the Pepsi-Cola bottling plant and a march by workers demanding union recognition at a St. Paul meatpacking plant, rubs his eyes and asks, "What's going on here?" When I arrive for work that day I salvage the newspaper from the trash can just outside the store entrance—which isn't difficult because the trash can is overflowing as usual and I don't have to dig down very far. Then I march that newspaper back to the break room, where I leave it face up on a table, in case anyone's missed the headline. This new role—bearer of really big news!—makes me feel busy and important. At ladies', I relate the news to Melissa, adding that the hotel workers already earn over a dollar an hour more than we do and that that hasn't stopped them from striking for more. She blinks a few times, considering, then Isabelle comes up and announces that the regional manager will be visiting our store tomorrow, so everything has to be "zoned to the nth degree." The day is upon us.

I have a lot more on my mind than the challenge of organizing the Faded Glory jeans shelves. At about six I'm supposed
to call two motels charging only $40 a day, where something
may have opened up, but I realize I've left the phone numbers
in the car. I don't want to use up any breaks fetching them—
not today, with the strike news to talk about. Do I dare engage
in some major time theft? And how can I get out without
Isabelle noticing? She's already caught me folding the jeans the
wrong way—you do them in thirds, with the ankles on the
inside, not on the outside—and has come by to check a second
time. It is, of all people, Howard who provides me with an out,
suddenly appearing at my side to inform me that I'm way
behind in my CBLs. New employees are supposed to make
their way through the CBL training modules by leaving the
floor with the permission of their supervisors, and I had been
doing so in a halfhearted way—getting through cardboard-box
opening, pallet loading, and trash compacting—until the program jammed. Now it's been fixed, he says, and I'm to get back
to the computer immediately. This gets me out of ladies' but
puts me a lot farther from the store exit. I apply myself to a
module in which Sam Walton waxes manic about the perpetual inventory system, then I cautiously get up from the computer to see if Howard is anywhere around. Good, the way is
clear. I am walking purposefully toward the front of the store
when I catch sight of him walking in the same direction, about
one hundred feet to my left. I dart into shoes, emerging to see
him still moving in a path parallel to mine. I dodge him again
by going into bras, then tacking right to the far side of ladies'.
I've seen this kind of thing in the movies, where the good guy
eludes the bad one in some kind of complicated public space,
but I never imagined doing it myself.

Back in the store with the numbers in my vest pocket, I decide to steal a few more minutes and make my calls on company time from the pay phone near layaway. The first motel doesn't answer, which is not uncommon in your low-rate places. On a whim I call Caroline to see if she's on strike: no, not her hotel. But she laughs as she tells me that last night on the TV news she saw a manager from the hotel where she used to work. He's a white guy who'd enjoyed reminding her that she was the first African American to be hired for anything above a housekeeping job and here he was on TV, reduced to pushing a broom while the regular broom pushers walked the picket line. I'm dialing the second motel when Howard reappears. Why aren't I at the computer? he wants to know, giving me his signature hate smile. "Break," I say, flashing him what is known to primatologists as a "fear grin"—half teeth baring and half grimace. If you're going to steal, you better be prepared to lie. He can find out in a minute, of course, by checking to see if I'm actually punched out. I could be written up, banished to bras, called in for a talking-to by a deeply disappointed Roberta. But the second motel has no room for another few days, which means that, for purely financial reasons, my career at Wal-Mart is about to come to a sudden end anyway.

When Melissa is getting ready to leave work at six, I tell her I'm quitting, possibly the next day. Well then, she thinks she'll be going too, because she doesn't want to work here without me. We both look at the floor. I understand that this is not a confession of love, just a practical consideration. You don't want to work with people who can't hold up their end or whom you don't like being with, and you don't want to keep readjusting to new ones. We exchange addresses, including my real and permanent one. I tell her about the book I'm working on and she nods, not particularly surprised, and says she hopes she hasn't said "too many bad things about Wal-Mart." I assure her that she hasn't and that she'll be well disguised anyway. Then she tells me she's been thinking about it, and $7 an hour isn't enough for how hard we work after all, and she's going to apply at a plastics factory where she hopes she can get $9.

At ten that night I go to the break room for my final break, too footsore to walk out to the smoking area, and sit down with my feet up on the bench. My earlier break, the one I'd committed so many crimes to preserve, had been a complete bust, with no other human around but a management-level woman from accounting. I have that late-shift shut-in feeling that there's no world beyond the doors, no problem greater than the mystery items remaining at the bottom of my cart. There's only one other person in the break room anyway, a white woman of maybe thirty, watching TV, and I don't have the energy to start a conversation, even with the rich topic of the strike at hand.

And then, by the grace of the God who dictated the Sermon on the Mount to Jesus, who watches over Melissa and sparrows everywhere, the TV picks up on the local news and the news is about the strike. A picketer with a little boy tells the camera, "This is for my son. I'm doing this for my son." Senator Paul Wellstone is standing there too. He shakes the boy's hand, and says, "You should be proud of your father." At this my sole companion jumps up, grinning, and waves a fist in the air at the TV set. I give her the rapid two-index-fingers-pointing-down signal that means "Here! Us! We could do that too!" She bounds over to where I'm sitting—if I were feeling peppier I would have gone over to her—leans into my face, and says, "Damn right!" I don't know whether it's my feet or the fact that she said "damn," or what, but I find myself tearing up. She talks well past my legal break time and possibly hers—about her daughter, how she's sick of working long hours and never getting enough time with her, and what does this lead to anyway, when you can't make enough to save?

I still think we could have done something, she and I, if I could have afforded to work at Wal-Mart a little longer.

Evaluation

How did I do as a low-wage worker? If I may begin with a brief round of applause: I didn't do half bad at the work itself, and I claim this as a considerable achievement. You might think that unskilled jobs would be a snap for someone who holds a Ph.D. and whose normal line of work requires learning entirely new things every couple of weeks. Not so. The first thing I discovered is that no job, no matter how lowly, is truly "unskilled." Every one of the six jobs I entered into in the course of this project required concentration, and most demanded that I master new terms, new tools, and new skills—from placing orders on restaurant computers to wielding the backpack vacuum cleaner. None of these things came as easily to me as I would have liked; no one ever said, "Wow, you're fast!" or "Can you believe she just started?" Whatever my accomplishments in the rest of my life, in the low-wage work world I was a person of average ability—capable of learning the job and also capable of screwing up.

I did have my moments of glory. There were days at The Maids when I got my own tasks finished fast enough that I was able to lighten the load on others, and I feel good about that. There was my breakthrough at Wal-Mart, where I truly believe that, if I'd been able to keep my mouth shut, I would have progressed in a year or two to a wage of $7.50 or more an hour. And I'll bask for the rest of my life in the memory of that day at the Woodcrest when I fed the locked Alzheimer's ward all by myself, cleaned up afterward, and even managed to extract a few smiles from the vacant faces of my charges in the process.

It's not just the work that has to be learned in each situation. Each job presents a self-contained social world, with its own personalities, hierarchy, customs, and standards. Sometimes I was given scraps of sociological data to work with, such as "Watch out for so-and-so, he's a real asshole." More commonly it was left to me to figure out such essentials as who was in charge, who was good to work with, who could take a joke. Here years of travel probably stood me in good stead, although in my normal life I usually enter new situations in some respected, even attention-getting role like "guest lecturer" or "workshop leader." It's a lot harder, I found, to sort out a human microsystem when you're looking up at it from the bottom, and, of course, a lot more necessary to do so.

Standards are another tricky issue. To be "good to work with" yourself, you need to be fast and thorough, but not so fast and thorough that you end up making things tougher for everyone else. There was seldom any danger of my raising the bar, but at the Hearthside Annette once upbraided me for freshening up the display desserts: "They'll expect us all to start doing that!" So I desisted, just as I would have slowed down to an arthritic pace in any job, in the event that a manager showed up to do a time-and-motion study. Similarly, at Wal-Mart, a coworker once advised me that, although I had a lot to learn, it was also important not to "know too much," or at least never to reveal one's full abilities to management, because "the more they think you can do, the more they'll use you and abuse you." My mentors in these matters were not lazy; they just understood that there are few or no rewards for heroic performance. The trick lies in figuring out how to budget your energy so there'll be some left over for the next day.

And all of these jobs were physically demanding, some of them even damaging if performed month after month. Now, I am an unusually fit person, with years of weight lifting and aerobics behind me, but I learned something that no one ever mentioned in the gym: that a lot of what we experience as strength comes from knowing what to do with weakness. You feel it coming on halfway through a shift or later, and you can interpret it the normal way as a symptom of a kind of low-level illness, curable with immediate rest. Or you can interpret it another way, as a reminder of the hard work you've done so far and hence as evidence of how much you are still capable of doing—in which case the exhaustion becomes a kind of splint, holding you up. Obviously there are limits to this form of self-delusion, and I would have reached mine quickly enough if I'd had to go home from my various jobs to chase toddlers and pick up after a family, as so many women do. But the fact that I survived physically, that in a time period well into my fifties I never collapsed or needed time off to recuperate, is something I am inordinately proud of.

Furthermore, I displayed, or usually displayed, all those traits deemed essential to job readiness: punctuality, cleanliness, cheerfulness, obedience. These are the qualities that welfare-to-work job-training programs often seek to inculcate, though I suspect that most welfare recipients already possess them, or would if their child care and transportation problems were solved. I was simply following the rules I had laid down for myself at the beginning of the project and doing the best I could to hold each job. Don't take my word for it: supervisors sometimes told me I was doing well—"fine" or even "great." So all in all, with some demerits for screwups and gold stars for effort, I think it's fair to say that as a worker, a jobholder, I deserve a B or maybe B+.

But the real question is not how well I did at work but how well I did at life in general, which includes eating and having a place to stay. The fact that these are two separate questions needs to be underscored right away. In the rhetorical buildup to welfare reform, it was uniformly assumed that a job was the ticket out of poverty and that the only thing holding back welfare recipients was their reluctance to get out and get one. I got one and sometimes more than one, but my track record in the survival department is far less admirable than my performance as a jobholder. On small things I was thrifty enough; no expenditures on "carousing," flashy clothes, or any of the other indulgences that are often smugly believed to undermine the budgets of the poor. True, the $30 slacks in Key West and the $20 belt in Minneapolis were extravagances; I now know I could have done better at the Salvation Army or even at Wal-Mart. Food, though, I pretty much got down to a science: lots of chopped meat, beans, cheese, and noodles when I had a kitchen to cook in; otherwise, fast food, which I was able to keep down to about $9 a day. But let's look at the record.

In Key West, I earned $1,039 in one month and spent $517 on food, gas, toiletries, laundry, phone, and utilities. Rent was the deal breaker. If I had remained in my $500 efficiency, I would have been able to pay the rent and have $22 left over (which is still $78 less than the cash I had in my pocket at the start of the month). This in itself would have been a dicey situation if I had attempted to continue for a few more months, because sooner or later I would have had to spend something on medical and dental care or drugs other than ibuprofen. But my move to the trailer park—for the purpose, you will recall, of taking a second job—made me responsible for $625 a month in rent alone, utilities not included. Here I might have economized by giving up the car and buying a used bike (for about $50) or walking to work. Still, two jobs, or at least a job and a half, would be a necessity, and I had learned that I could not do two physically demanding jobs in the same day, at least not at any acceptable standard of performance.

In Portland, Maine, I came closest to achieving a decent fit between income and expenses, but only because I worked seven days a week. Between my two jobs, I was earning approximately $300 a week after taxes and paying $480 a month in rent, or a manageable 40 percent of my earnings. It helped, too, that gas and electricity were included in my rent and that I got two or three free meals each weekend at the nursing home. But I was there at the beginning of the off-season. If I had stayed until June 2000 I would have faced the Blue Haven's summer rent of $390 a week, which would of course have been out of the question. So to survive year-round, I would have had to save enough, in the months between August 1999 and May 2000, to accumulate the first month's rent and deposit on an actual apartment. I think I could have done this—saved $800 to $1,000—at least if no car trouble or illness interfered with my budget. I am not sure, however, that I could have maintained the seven-day-a-week regimen month after month or eluded the kinds of injuries that afflicted my fellow workers in the housecleaning business.

In Minneapolis—well, here we are left with a lot of speculation. If I had been able to find an apartment for $400 a month or less, my pay at Wal-Mart—$1,120 a month before taxes—might have been sufficient, although the cost of living in a motel while I searched for such an apartment might have made it impossible for me to save enough for the first month's rent and deposit. A weekend job, such as the one I almost landed at a supermarket for about $7.75 an hour, would have helped, but I had no guarantee that I could arrange my schedule at Wal-Mart to reliably exclude weekends. If I had taken the job at Menards and the pay was in fact $10 an hour for eleven hours a day, I would have made about $440 a week after taxes— enough to pay for a motel room and still have something left over to save up for the initial costs of an apartment. But were they really offering $10 an hour? And could I have stayed on my feet eleven hours a day, five days a week? So yes, with some different choices, I probably could have survived in Minneapolis. But I'm not going back for a rematch.

All right, I made mistakes, especially in Minneapolis, and these mistakes were at the time an occasion for feelings of failure and shame. I should have pulled myself together and taken the better-paying job; I should have moved into the dormitory I finally found (although at $19 a night, even a dorm bed would have been a luxury on Wal-Mart wages). But it must be said in my defense that plenty of other people were making the same mistakes: working at Wal-Mart rather than at one of the better-paying jobs available (often, I assume, because of transportation problems); living in residential motels at $200 to $300 a week. So the problem goes beyond my personal failings and miscalculations. Something is wrong, very wrong, when a single person in good health, a person who in addition possesses a working car, can barely support herself by the sweat of her brow. You don't need a degree in economics to see that wages are too low and rents too high.

THE PROBLEM OF RENTS IS EASY FOR A NONECONOMIST, EVEN A sparsely educated low-wage worker, to grasp: it's the market, stupid. When the rich and the poor compete for housing on the open market, the poor don't stand a chance. The rich can always outbid them, buy up their tenements or trailer parks, and replace them with condos, McMansions, golf courses, or whatever they like. Since the rich have become more numerous, thanks largely to rising stock prices and executive salaries, the poor have necessarily been forced into housing that is more expensive, more dilapidated, or more distant from their places of work. Recall that in Key West, the trailer park convenient to hotel jobs was charging $625 a month for a half-size trailer, forcing low-wage workers to search for housing farther and farther away in less fashionable keys. But rents were also sky-rocketing in the touristically challenged city of Minneapolis, where the last bits of near-affordable housing lie deep in the city, while job growth has occurred on the city's periphery, next to distinctly unaffordable suburbs. Insofar as the poor have to work near the dwellings of the rich—as in the case of so many service and retail jobs—they are stuck with lengthy commutes or dauntingly expensive housing.

If there seems to be general complacency about the low-income housing crisis, this is partly because it is in no way reflected in the official poverty rate, which has remained for the past several years at a soothingly low 13 percent or so. The reason for the disconnect between the actual housing nightmare of the poor and "poverty," as officially defined, is simple: the official poverty level is still calculated by the archaic method of taking the bare-bones cost of food for a family of a given size and multiplying this number by three. Yet food is relatively inflation-proof, at least compared with rent. In the early 1960s, when this method of calculating poverty was devised, food accounted for 24 percent of the average family budget (not 33 percent even then, it should be noted) and housing 29 percent. In 1999, food took up only 16 percent of the family budget, while housing had soared to 37 percent.[1] So the choice of food as the basis for calculating family budgets seems fairly arbitrary today; we might as well abolish poverty altogether, at least on paper, by defining a subsistence budget as some multiple of average expenditures on comic books or dental floss.

When the market fails to distribute some vital commodity, such as housing, to all who require it, the usual liberal-to-moderate expectation is that the government will step in and help. We accept this principle—at least in a halfhearted and faltering way—in the case of health care, where government

[1] Jared Bernstein, Chauna Brocht, and Maggie Spade-Aguilar, "How Much Is Enough? Basic Family Budgets for Working Families," Economic Policy Institute, Washington, D.C., 2000, p. 14.

offers Medicare to the elderly, Medicaid to the desperately poor, and various state programs to the children of the merely very poor. But in the case of housing, the extreme upward skewing of the market has been accompanied by a cowardly public sector retreat from responsibility. Expenditures on public housing have fallen since the 1980s, and the expansion of public rental subsidies came to a halt in the mid-1990s. At the same time, housing subsidies for home owners—who tend to be far more affluent than renters—have remained at their usual munificent levels. It did not escape my attention, as a temporarily low-income person, that the housing subsidy I normally receive in my real life—over $20,000 a year in the form of a mortgage-interest deduction—would have allowed a truly low-income family to live in relative splendor. Had this amount been available to me in monthly installments in Minneapolis, I could have moved into one of those "executive" condos with sauna, health club, and pool.

But if rents are exquisitely sensitive to market forces, wages clearly are not. Every city where I worked in the course of this project was experiencing what local businesspeople defined as a "labor shortage"—commented on in the local press and revealed by the ubiquitous signs saying "Now Hiring" or, more imperiously, "We Are Now Accepting Applications." Yet wages for people near the bottom of the labor market remain fairly flat, even "stagnant." "Certainly," the *New York Times* reported in March 2000, "inflationary wage gains are not evident in national wage statistics."[2] Federal Reserve chief Alan Greenspan, who spends much of his time anxiously scanning

[2] "Companies Try Dipping Deeper into Labor Pool," *New York Times,* March 26, 2000.

the horizon for the slightest hint of such "inflationary" gains, was pleased to inform Congress in July 2000 that the forecast seemed largely trouble-free. He went so far as to suggest that the economic laws linking low unemployment to wage increases may no longer be operative, which is a little like saying that the law of supply and demand has been repealed.[3] Some economists argue that the apparent paradox rests on an illusion: there is no real "labor shortage," only a shortage of people willing to work at the wages currently being offered.[4] You might as well talk about a "Lexus shortage"—which there is, in a sense, for anyone unwilling to pay $40,000 for a car.

In fact, wages *have* risen, or did rise, anyway, between 1996 and 1999. When I called around to various economists in the summer of 2000 and complained about the inadequacy of the wages available to entry-level workers, this was their first response: "But wages are going up!" According to the Economic Policy Institute, the poorest 10 percent of American workers saw their wages rise from $5.49 an hour (in 1999 dollars) in 1996 to $6.05 in 1999. Moving up the socioeconomic ladder, the next 10 percent–sized slice of Americans—which is roughly where I found myself as a low-wage worker—went from $6.80 an hour in 1996 to $7.35 in 1999.[5]

Obviously we have one of those debates over whether the glass is half empty or half full; the increases that seem to have mollified many economists do not seem so impressive to me.

[3] "An Epitaph for a Rule That Just Won't Die," *New York Times,* July 30, 2000.
[4] "Fact or Fallacy: Labor Shortage May Really Be Wage Stagnation," *Chicago Tribune,* July 2, 2000; "It's a Wage Shortage, Not a Labor Shortage," *Minneapolis Star Tribune,* March 25, 2000.
[5] I thank John Schmidt at the Economic Policy Institute in Washington, D.C., for preparing the wage data for me.

To put the wage gains of the past four years in somewhat dismal perspective: they have not been sufficient to bring low-wage workers up to the amounts they were earning twenty-seven years ago, in 1973. In the first quarter of 2000, the poorest 10 percent of workers were earning only 91 percent of what they earned in the distant era of Watergate and disco music. Furthermore, of all workers, the poorest have made the least progress back to their 1973 wage levels. Relatively well-off workers in the eighth decile, or 10 percent–sized slice, where earnings are about $20 an hour, are now making 106.6 percent of what they earned in 1973. When I persisted in my carping to the economists, they generally backed down a bit, conceding that while wages at the bottom are going up, they're not going up very briskly. Lawrence Michel at the Economic Policy Institute, who had at the beginning of our conversation taken the half-full perspective, heightened the mystery when he observed that productivity—to which wages are theoretically tied—has been rising at such a healthy clip that "workers should be getting much more."[6]

The most obvious reason why they're not is that employers resist wage increases with every trick they can think of and every ounce of strength they can summon. I had an opportunity to query one of my own employers on this subject in Maine. You may remember the time when Ted, my boss at The Maids, drove me about forty minutes to a house where I was needed to reinforce a shorthanded team. In the course of complaining about his hard lot in life, he avowed that he could double his business overnight if only he could find enough reliable workers. As politely as possible, I asked him why he didn't

[6] Interview, July 18, 2000.

just raise the pay. The question seemed to slide right off him. We offer "mothers' hours," he told me, meaning that the workday was supposedly over at three—as if to say, "With a benefit like that, how could anybody complain about wages?"

In fact, I suspect that the free breakfast he provided us represented the only concession to the labor shortage that he was prepared to make. Similarly, the Wal-Mart where I worked was offering free doughnuts once a week to any employees who could arrange to take their breaks while the supply lasted. As Louis Uchitelle has reported in the *New York Times,* many employers will offer almost anything—free meals, subsidized transportation, store discounts—rather than raise wages. The reason for this, in the words of one employer, is that such extras "can be shed more easily" than wage increases when changes in the market seem to make them unnecessary.[7] In the same spirit, automobile manufacturers would rather offer their customers cash rebates than reduced prices; the advantage of the rebate is that it seems like a gift and can be withdrawn without explanation.

But the resistance of employers only raises a second and ultimately more intractable question: Why isn't this resistance met by more effective counterpressure from the workers themselves? In evading and warding off wage increases, employers are of course behaving in an economically rational fashion; their business isn't to make their employees more comfortable and secure but to maximize the bottom line. So why don't employees behave in an equally rational fashion, demanding higher wages of their employers or seeking out better-paying

[7] "Companies Try Dipping Deeper into Labor Pool," *New York Times,* March 26, 2000.

jobs? The assumption behind the law of supply and demand, as it applies to labor, is that workers will sort themselves out as effectively as marbles on an inclined plane—gravitating to the better-paying jobs and either leaving the recalcitrant employers behind or forcing them to up the pay. "Economic man," that great abstraction of economic science, is supposed to do whatever it takes, within certain limits, to maximize his economic advantage.

I was baffled, initially, by what seemed like a certain lack of get-up-and-go on the part of my fellow workers. Why didn't they just leave for a better-paying job, as I did when I moved from the Hearthside to Jerry's? Part of the answer is that actual humans experience a little more "friction" than marbles do, and the poorer they are, the more constrained their mobility usually is. Low-wage people who don't have cars are often dependent on a relative who is willing to drop them off and pick them up again each day, sometimes on a route that includes the babysitter's house or the child care center. Change your place of work and you may be confronted with an impossible topographical problem to solve, or at least a reluctant driver to persuade. Some of my coworkers, in Minneapolis as well as Key West, rode bikes to work, and this clearly limited their geographical range. For those who do possess cars, there is still the problem of gas prices, not to mention the general hassle, which is of course far more onerous for the carless, of getting around to fill out applications, to be interviewed, to take drug tests. I have mentioned, too, the general reluctance to exchange the devil you know for one that you don't know, even when the latter is tempting you with a better wage-benefit package. At each new job, you have to start all over, clueless and friendless.

There is another way that low-income workers differ from "economic man." For the laws of economics to work, the "players" need to be well informed about their options. The ideal case—and I've read that the technology for this is just around the corner—would be the consumer whose Palm Pilot displays the menu and prices for every restaurant or store he or she passes. Even without such technological assistance, affluent job hunters expect to study the salary-benefit packages offered by their potential employers, watch the financial news to find out if these packages are in line with those being offered in other regions or fields, and probably do a little bargaining before taking a job.

But there are no Palm Pilots, cable channels, or Web sites to advise the low-wage job seeker. She has only the help-wanted signs and the want ads to go on, and most of these coyly refrain from mentioning numbers. So information about who earns what and where has to travel by word of mouth, and for inexplicable cultural reasons, this is a very slow and unreliable route. Twin Cities job market analyst Kristine Jacobs pinpoints what she calls the "money taboo" as a major factor preventing workers from optimizing their earnings. "There's a code of silence surrounding issues related to individuals' earnings," she told me. "We confess everything else in our society—sex, crime, illness. But no one wants to reveal what they earn or how they got it. The money taboo is the one thing that employers can always count on."[8] I suspect that this "taboo" operates most effectively among the lowest-paid people, because, in a society that endlessly celebrates its dot-com billionaires and centimillionaire athletes, $7 or even $10 an hour

---

[8] Personal communication, July 24, 2000.

can feel like a mark of innate inferiority. So you may or may not find out that, say, the Target down the road is paying better than Wal-Mart, even if you have a sister-in-law working there.

Employers, of course, do little to encourage the economic literacy of their workers. They may exhort potential customers to "Compare Our Prices!" but they're not eager to have workers do the same with wages. I have mentioned the way the hiring process seems designed, in some cases, to prevent any discussion or even disclosure of wages—whisking the applicant from interview to orientation before the crass subject of money can be raised. Some employers go further; instead of relying on the informal "money taboo" to keep workers from discussing and comparing wages, they specifically enjoin workers from doing so. The *New York Times* recently reported on several lawsuits brought by employees who had allegedly been fired for breaking this rule—a woman, for example, who asked for higher pay after learning from her male coworkers that she was being paid considerably less than they were for the very same work. The National Labor Relations Act of 1935 makes it illegal to punish people for revealing their wages to one another, but the practice is likely to persist until rooted out by lawsuits, company by company.[9]

BUT IF IT'S HARD FOR WORKERS TO OBEY THE LAWS OF ECONOMICS by examining their options and moving on to better jobs, why don't more of them take a stand where they are—demanding better wages and work conditions, either individually or as a group? This is a huge question, probably the subject of many a

[9] "The Biggest Company Secret: Workers Challenge Employer Practices on Pay Confidentiality," *New York Times,* July 28, 2000.

dissertation in the field of industrial psychology, and here I can only comment on the things I observed. One of these was the co-optative power of management, illustrated by such euphemisms as *associate* and *team member*. At The Maids, the boss—who, as the only male in our midst, exerted a creepy, paternalistic kind of power—had managed to convince some of my coworkers that he was struggling against difficult odds and deserving of their unstinting forbearance. Wal-Mart has a number of more impersonal and probably more effective ways of getting its workers to feel like "associates." There was the profit-sharing plan, with Wal-Mart's stock price posted daily in a prominent spot near the break room. There was the company's much-heralded patriotism, evidenced in the banners over the shopping floor urging workers and customers to contribute to the construction of a World War II veterans' memorial (Sam Walton having been one of them). There were "associate" meetings that served as pep rallies, complete with the Wal-Mart cheer: "Gimme a 'W,'" etc.

The chance to identify with a powerful and wealthy entity—the company or the boss—is only the carrot. There is also a stick. What surprised and offended me most about the low-wage workplace (and yes, here all my middle-class privilege is on full display) was the extent to which one is required to surrender one's basic civil rights and—what boils down to the same thing—self-respect. I learned this at the very beginning of my stint as a waitress, when I was warned that my purse could be searched by management at any time. I wasn't carrying stolen salt shakers or anything else of a compromising nature, but still, there's something about the prospect of a purse search that makes a woman feel a few buttons short of fully dressed. After work, I called around and found that this practice is entirely legal: if the purse is on the boss's property—which of course it was—the boss has the right to examine its contents.

Drug testing is another routine indignity. Civil libertarians see it as a violation of our Fourth Amendment freedom from "unreasonable search"; most jobholders and applicants find it simply embarrassing. In some testing protocols, the employee has to strip to her underwear and pee into a cup in the presence of an aide or technician. Mercifully, I got to keep my clothes on and shut the toilet stall door behind me, but even so, urination is a private act and it is degrading to have to perform it at the command of some powerful other. I would add pre-employment personality tests to the list of demeaning intrusions, or at least much of their usual content. Maybe the hypothetical types of questions can be justified—whether you would steal if an opportunity arose or turn in a thieving coworker and so on—but not questions about your "moods of self-pity," whether you are a loner or believe you are usually misunderstood. It is unsettling, at the very least, to give a stranger access to things, like your self-doubts and your urine, that are otherwise shared only in medical or therapeutic situations.

There are other, more direct ways of keeping low-wage employees in their place. Rules against "gossip," or even "talking," make it hard to air your grievances to peers or—should you be so daring—to enlist other workers in a group effort to bring about change, through a union organizing drive, for example. Those who do step out of line often face little unexplained punishments, such as having their schedules or their work assignments unilaterally changed. Or you may be fired; those low-wage workers who work without union contracts, which is the great majority of them, work "at will," meaning at the will of the employer, and are subject to dismissal without explanation. The AFL-CIO estimates that ten thousand workers a year are fired for participating in union organizing drives, and since it is illegal to fire people for union activity, I suspect that these firings are usually justified in terms of unrelated minor infractions. Wal-Mart employees who have bucked the company—by getting involved in a unionization drive or by suing the company for failing to pay overtime—have been fired for breaking the company rule against using profanity.[10]

So if low-wage workers do not always behave in an economically rational way, that is, as free agents within a capitalist democracy, it is because they dwell in a place that is neither free nor in any way democratic. When you enter the low-wage workplace—and many of the medium-wage workplaces as well—you check your civil liberties at the door, leave America and all it supposedly stands for behind, and learn to zip your lips for the duration of the shift. The consequences of this routine surrender go beyond the issues of wages and poverty. We can hardly pride ourselves on being the world's preeminent democracy, after all, if large numbers of citizens spend half their waking hours in what amounts, in plain terms, to a dictatorship.

Any dictatorship takes a psychological toll on its subjects. If you are treated as an untrustworthy person—a potential slacker, drug addict, or thief—you may begin to feel less trustworthy yourself. If you are constantly reminded of your lowly position in the social hierarchy, whether by individual managers or by a plethora of impersonal rules, you begin to accept that unfortunate status. To draw for a moment from an entirely

---

[10] Bob Ortega, *In Sam We Trust,* p. 356; "Former Wal-Mart Workers File Overtime Suit in Harrison County," *Charleston Gazette,* January 24, 1999.

different corner of my life, that part of me still attached to the biological sciences, there is ample evidence that animals—rats and monkeys, for example—that are forced into a subordinate status within their social systems adapt their brain chemistry accordingly, becoming "depressed" in humanlike ways. Their behavior is anxious and withdrawn; the level of serotonin (the neurotransmitter boosted by some antidepressants) declines in their brains. And—what is especially relevant here—they avoid fighting even in self-defense.[11]

Humans are, of course, vastly more complicated; even in situations of extreme subordination, we can pump up our self-esteem with thoughts of our families, our religion, our hopes for the future. But as much as any other social animal, and more so than many, we depend for our self-image on the humans immediately around us—to the point of altering our perceptions of the world so as to fit in with theirs.[12] My guess is that the indignities imposed on so many low-wage workers—the drug tests, the constant surveillance, being "reamed out" by managers—are part of what keeps wages low. If you're made to feel unworthy enough, you may come to think that what you're paid is what you are actually worth.

It is hard to imagine any other function for workplace authoritarianism. Managers may truly believe that, without their unremitting efforts, all work would quickly grind to a

[11] See, for example, C. A. Shively, K. Laber-Laird, and R. F. Anton, "Behavior and Physiology of Social Stress and Depression in Female Cynomolgous Monkeys," *Biological Psychiatry* 41:8 (1997), pp. 871–82, and D. C. Blanchard et al., "Visible Burrow System as a Model of Chronic Social Stress: Behavioral and Neuroendocrine Correlates," *Psychoneuroendocrinology* 20:2 (1995), pp. 117–34.

[12] See, for example, chapter 7, "Conformity," in David G. Myers, *Social Psychology* (McGraw-Hill, 1987).

halt. That is not my impression. While I encountered some cynics and plenty of people who had learned to budget their energy, I never met an actual slacker or, for that matter, a drug addict or thief. On the contrary, I was amazed and sometimes saddened by the pride people took in jobs that rewarded them so meagerly, either in wages or in recognition. Often, in fact, these people experienced management as an obstacle to getting the job done as it should be done. Waitresses chafed at managers' stinginess toward the customers; housecleaners resented the time constraints that sometimes made them cut corners; retail workers wanted the floor to be beautiful, not cluttered with excess stock as management required. Left to themselves, they devised systems of cooperation and work sharing; when there was a crisis, they rose to it. In fact, it was often hard to see what the function of management was, other than to exact obeisance.

There seems to be a vicious cycle at work here, making ours not just an economy but a culture of extreme inequality. Corporate decision makers, and even some two-bit entrepreneurs like my boss at The Maids, occupy an economic position miles above that of the underpaid people whose labor they depend on. For reasons that have more to do with class—and often racial—prejudice than with actual experience, they tend to fear and distrust the category of people from which they recruit their workers. Hence the perceived need for repressive management and intrusive measures like drug and personality testing. But these things cost money—$20,000 or more a year for a manager, $100 a pop for a drug test, and so on—and the high cost of repression results in ever more pressure to hold wages down. The larger society seems to be caught up in a similar cycle: cutting public services for the poor, which are sometimes referred to collectively as the "social wage," while investing ever more heavily in prisons and cops. And in the larger society, too, the cost of repression becomes another factor weighing against the expansion or restoration of needed services. It is a tragic cycle, condemning us to ever deeper inequality, and in the long run, almost no one benefits but the agents of repression themselves.

But whatever keeps wages low—and I'm sure my comments have barely scratched the surface—the result is that many people earn far less than they need to live on. How much is that? The Economic Policy Institute recently reviewed dozens of studies of what constitutes a "living wage" and came up with an average figure of $30,000 a year for a family of one adult and two children, which amounts to a wage of $14 an hour. This is not the very minimum such a family could live on; the budget includes health insurance, a telephone, and child care at a licensed center, for example, which are well beyond the reach of millions. But it does not include restaurant meals, video rentals, Internet access, wine and liquor, cigarettes and lottery tickets, or even very much meat. The shocking thing is that the majority of American workers, about 60 percent, earn less than $14 an hour. Many of them get by by teaming up with another wage earner, a spouse or grown child. Some draw on government help in the form of food stamps, housing vouchers, the earned income tax credit, or—for those coming off welfare in relatively generous states—subsidized child care. But others—single mothers for example—have nothing but their own wages to live on, no matter how many mouths there are to feed.

Employers will look at that $30,000 figure, which is over twice what they currently pay entry-level workers, and see nothing but bankruptcy ahead. Indeed, it is probably impossible for the private sector to provide everyone with an adequate standard of living through wages, or even wages plus benefits, alone: too much of what we need, such as reliable child care, is just too expensive, even for middle-class families. Most civilized nations compensate for the inadequacy of wages by providing relatively generous public services such as health insurance, free or subsidized child care, subsidized housing, and effective public transportation. But the United States, for all its wealth, leaves its citizens to fend for themselves—facing market-based rents, for example, on their wages alone. For millions of Americans, that $10—or even $8 or $6—hourly wage is all there is.

It is common, among the nonpoor, to think of poverty as a sustainable condition—austere, perhaps, but they get by somehow, don't they? They are "always with us." What is harder for the nonpoor to see is poverty as acute distress: The lunch that consists of Doritos or hot dog rolls, leading to faintness before the end of the shift. The "home" that is also a car or a van. The illness or injury that must be "worked through," with gritted teeth, because there's no sick pay or health insurance and the loss of one day's pay will mean no groceries for the next. These experiences are not part of a sustainable lifestyle, even a lifestyle of chronic deprivation and relentless low-level punishment. They are, by almost any standard of subsistence, emergency situations. And that is how we should see the poverty of so many millions of low-wage Americans—as a state of emergency.

IN THE SUMMER OF 2000 I RETURNED—PERMANENTLY, I HAVE EVERY reason to hope—to my customary place in the socioeconomic spectrum. I go to restaurants, often far finer ones than the places where I worked, and sit down at a table. I sleep in hotel rooms that someone else has cleaned and shop in stores that others will tidy when I leave. To go from the bottom 20 percent to the top 20 percent is to enter a magical world where needs are met, problems are solved, almost without any intermediate effort. If you want to get somewhere fast, you hail a cab. If your aged parents have grown tiresome or incontinent, you put them away where others will deal with their dirty diapers and dementia. If you are part of the upper-middle-class majority that employs a maid or maid service, you return from work to find the house miraculously restored to order—the toilet bowls shit-free and gleaming, the socks that you left on the floor levitated back to their normal dwelling place. Here, sweat is a metaphor for hard work, but seldom its consequence. Hundreds of little things get done, reliably and routinely every day, without anyone's seeming to do them.

The top 20 percent routinely exercises other, far more consequential forms of power in the world. This stratum, which contains what I have termed in an earlier book the "professional-managerial class," is the home of our decision makers, opinion shapers, culture creators—our professors, lawyers, executives, entertainers, politicians, judges, writers, producers, and editors.[13] When they speak, they are listened to. When they complain, someone usually scurries to correct the problem and apologize for it. If they complain often enough, someone far below them in wealth and influence may be chastised or even fired. Political power, too, is concentrated within the top 20 percent, since its members are far more likely than the poor—or even the middle class—to discern the all-too-tiny

[13] *Fear of Falling: The Inner Life of the Middle Class* (Pantheon, 1989).

distinctions between candidates that can make it seem worth-
while to contribute, participate, and vote. In all these ways, the
affluent exert inordinate power over the lives of the less affluent, and especially over the lives of the poor, determining what
public services will be available, if any, what minimum wage,
what laws governing the treatment of labor.

So it is alarming, upon returning to the upper middle class
from a sojourn, however artificial and temporary, among the
poor, to find the rabbit hole close so suddenly and completely
behind me. You were *where,* doing *what?* Some odd optical
property of our highly polarized and unequal society makes the
poor almost invisible to their economic superiors. The poor
can see the affluent easily enough—on television, for example,
or on the covers of magazines. But the affluent rarely see the
poor or, if they do catch sight of them in some public space,
rarely know what they're seeing, since—thanks to consignment
stores and, yes, Wal-Mart—the poor are usually able to dis-
guise themselves as members of the more comfortable classes.
Forty years ago the hot journalistic topic was the "discovery of
the poor" in their inner-city and Appalachian "pockets of
poverty." Today you are more likely to find commentary on
their "disappearance," either as a supposed demographic reality or as a shortcoming of the middle-class imagination.

In a 2000 article on the "disappearing poor," journalist
James Fallows reports that, from the vantage point of the Internet's nouveaux riches, it is "hard to understand people for
whom a million dollars would be a fortune . . . not to mention
those for whom $246 is a full week's earnings."[14] Among the
reasons he and others have cited for the blindness of the afflu-

---

[14] "The Invisible Poor," *New York Times Magazine,* March 19, 2000.

ent is the fact that they are less and less likely to share spaces and services with the poor. As public schools and other public services deteriorate, those who can afford to do so send their children to private schools and spend their off-hours in private spaces—health clubs, for example, instead of the local park. They don't ride on public buses and subways. They withdraw from mixed neighborhoods into distant suburbs, gated communities, or guarded apartment towers; they shop in stores that, in line with the prevailing "market segmentation," are designed to appeal to the affluent alone. Even the affluent young are increasingly unlikely to spend their summers learning how the "other half" lives, as lifeguards, waitresses, or housekeepers at resort hotels. The *New York Times* reports that they now prefer career-relevant activities like summer school or interning in an appropriate professional setting to the "sweaty, low-paid and mind-numbing slots that have long been their lot."[15]

Then, too, the particular political moment favors what almost looks like a "conspiracy of silence" on the subject of poverty and the poor. The Democrats are not eager to find flaws in the period of "unprecedented prosperity" they take credit for; the Republicans have lost interest in the poor now that "welfare-as-we-know-it" has ended. Welfare reform itself is a factor weighing against any close investigation of the conditions of the poor. Both parties heartily endorsed it, and to acknowledge that low-wage work doesn't lift people out of poverty would be to admit that it may have been, in human terms, a catastrophic mistake. In fact, very little is known about

[15] "Summer Work Is Out of Favor with the Young," *New York Times,* June 18, 2000.

the fate of former welfare recipients because the 1996 welfare reform legislation blithely failed to include any provision for monitoring their postwelfare economic condition. Media accounts persistently bright-side the situation, highlighting the occasional success stories and downplaying the acknowledged increase in hunger.[16] And sometimes there seems to be almost deliberate deception. In June 2000, the press rushed to hail a study supposedly showing that Minnesota's welfare-to-work program had sharply reduced poverty and was, as *Time* magazine put it, a "winner."[17] Overlooked in these reports was the fact that the program in question was a pilot project that offered far more generous child care and other subsidies than Minnesota's actual welfare reform program. Perhaps the error can be forgiven—the pilot project, which ended in 1997, had the same name, Minnesota Family Investment Program, as Minnesota's much larger, ongoing welfare reform program.[18]

You would have to read a great many newspapers very carefully, cover to cover, to see the signs of distress. You would find, for example, that in 1999 Massachusetts food pantries reported a 72 percent increase in the demand for their services over the previous year, that Texas food banks were "scrounging" for food, despite donations at or above 1998 levels, as were those in Atlanta.[19] You might learn that in San Diego the Catholic Church could no longer, as of January 2000, accept

---

[16] The *National Journal* reports that the "good news" is that almost six million people have left the welfare rolls since 1996, while the "rest of the story" includes the problem that "these people sometimes don't have enough to eat" ("Welfare Reform, Act 2," June 24, 2000, pp. 1,978–93).

[17] "Minnesota's Welfare Reform Proves a Winner," *Time,* June 12, 2000.

[18] Center for Law and Social Policy, "Update," Washington, D.C., June 2000.

[19] "Study: More Go Hungry since Welfare Reform," *Boston Herald,* January 21, 2000; "Charity Can't Feed All while Welfare Reforms Implemented," *Houston*

homeless families at its shelter, which happens to be the city's largest, because it was already operating at twice its normal capacity.[20] You would come across news of a study showing that the percentage of Wisconsin food-stamp families in "extreme poverty"—defined as less than 50 percent of the federal poverty line—has tripled in the last decade to more than 30 percent.[21] You might discover that, nationwide, America's food banks are experiencing "a torrent of need which [they] cannot meet" and that, according to a survey conducted by the U.S. Conference of Mayors, 67 percent of the adults requesting emergency food aid are people with jobs.[22]

One reason nobody bothers to pull all these stories together and announce a widespread state of emergency may be that Americans of the newspaper-reading professional middle class are used to thinking of poverty as a consequence of unemployment. During the heyday of downsizing in the Reagan years, it very often was, and it still is for many inner-city residents who have no way of getting to the proliferating entry-level jobs on urban peripheries. When unemployment causes poverty, we know how to state the problem—typically, "the economy isn't growing fast enough"—and we know what the traditional liberal solution is—"full employment." But when we have full or nearly full employment, when jobs are available to any job

Chronicle, January 10, 2000; "Hunger Grows as Food Banks Try to Keep Pace," *Atlanta Journal and Constitution,* November 26, 1999.

[20] "Rise in Homeless Families Strains San Diego Aid," *Los Angeles Times,* January 24, 2000.

[21] "Hunger Problems Said to Be Getting Worse," *Milwaukee Journal Sentinel,* December 15, 1999.

[22] Deborah Leff, the president and CEO of the hunger-relief organization America's Second Harvest, quoted in the *National Journal,* op. cit.; "Hunger Persists in U.S. despite the Good Times," *Detroit News,* June 15, 2000.

seeker who can get to them, then the problem goes deeper and begins to cut into that web of expectations that make up the "social contract." According to a recent poll conducted by Jobs for the Future, a Boston-based employment research firm, 94 percent of Americans agree that "people who work full-time should be able to earn enough to keep their families out of poverty."[23] I grew up hearing over and over, to the point of tedium, that "hard work" was the secret of success: "Work hard and you'll get ahead" or "It's hard work that got us where we are." No one ever said that you could work hard—harder even than you ever thought possible—and still find yourself sinking ever deeper into poverty and debt.

When poor single mothers had the option of remaining out of the labor force on welfare, the middle and upper middle class tended to view them with a certain impatience, if not disgust. The welfare poor were excoriated for their laziness, their persistence in reproducing in unfavorable circumstances, their presumed addictions, and above all for their "dependency." Here they were, content to live off "government handouts" instead of seeking "self-sufficiency," like everyone else, through a job. They needed to get their act together, learn how to wind an alarm clock, get out there and get to work. But now that government has largely withdrawn its "handouts," now that the overwhelming majority of the poor are out there toiling in Wal-Mart or Wendy's—well, what are we to think of them? Disapproval and condescension no longer apply, so what outlook makes sense?

[23] "A National Survey of American Attitudes toward Low-Wage Workers and Welfare Reform," Jobs for the Future, Boston, May 24, 2000.

Guilt, you may be thinking warily. Isn't that what we're supposed to feel? But guilt doesn't go anywhere near far enough; the appropriate emotion is shame—shame at our *own* dependency, in this case, on the underpaid labor of others. When someone works for less pay than she can live on—when, for example, she goes hungry so that you can eat more cheaply and conveniently—then she has made a great sacrifice for you, she has made you a gift of some part of her abilities, her health, and her life. The "working poor," as they are approvingly termed, are in fact the major philanthropists of our society. They neglect their own children so that the children of others will be cared for; they live in substandard housing so that other homes will be shiny and perfect; they endure privation so that inflation will be low and stock prices high. To be a member of the working poor is to be an anonymous donor, a nameless benefactor, to everyone else. As Gail, one of my restaurant coworkers put it, "you give and you give."

Someday, of course—and I will make no predictions as to exactly when—they are bound to tire of getting so little in return and to demand to be paid what they're worth. There'll be a lot of anger when that day comes, and strikes and disruption. But the sky will not fall, and we will all be better off for it in the end.

Afterword: Nickel and Dimed

I completed the manuscript for this book in a time of seemingly boundless prosperity. Technology innovators and venture capitalists were acquiring sudden fortunes, buying up McMansions like the ones I had cleaned in Maine and much larger. Even secretaries in some hi-tech firms were striking it rich with their stock options. There was loose talk about a permanent conquest of the business cycle, and a sassy new spirit infecting American capitalism. In San Francisco, a billboard for an e-trading firm proclaimed, "Make love not war," and then—down at the bottom—"Screw it, just make money."

When *Nickel and Dimed* was published in May 2001, cracks were appearing in the dot-com bubble and the stock market had begun to falter, but the book still evidently came as a surprise, even a revelation, to many. Again and again, in that first year or two after publication, people came up to me and opened with the words, "I never thought . . ." or "I hadn't realized . . ." To my own amazement, *Nickel and Dimed* quickly ascended to the bestseller list and began winning awards— and I am particularly proud of the Christopher Award, from a Catholic group, for books that "affirm the highest values of the human spirit." The book inspired an A&E documentary called *Wage Slaves* and was transformed by playwright Joan Holden into a fast, funny play that has been performed in major theaters as well as many smaller venues throughout the country. It has been adopted as a "community read" in dozens of communities, including Rochester, Minnesota; Appleton, Wisconsin; Concord, New Hampshire; and Peoria, Illinois.

Criticisms, too, have accumulated over the years. In 2006, Adam Shepard, a recent graduate who had been forced to read *Nickel and Dimed* in college, undertook to refute it with his own experiment as a low-wage worker. He turned out to be far more financially successful than I had been, ending up, after ten months, with an apartment and several thousand dollars saved. It should be pointed out, however, that he spent his first seventy days living off of charity in a homeless shelter that also offered meals, a strategy that provided him with a considerable subsidy. He also enjoyed the advantage of being male, which meant he could work in industries such as moving and construction that pay better than the kinds of jobs that were open to me. But in his book, *Scratch Beginnings,* Shepard accused me, somewhat unchivalrously I think, of lacking the motivation to succeed.

A more common criticism is that *Nickel and Dimed* harbors a deep prejudice against Christians. This, anyway, has been one interpretation of the tent revival scene in Maine and my criticism of "visible Christians"—wearing Christian-themed T-shirts or "WWJD" bracelets—who tipped so poorly in Florida. Well, let me say that as an admirer of the Jesus of the Book of Matthew, I hold Christians to a pretty high standard. Rather than just appealing for donations, the tent revival preachers should have acknowledged the poverty of their audience. And when confronted with a server earning $2 and change an hour, the answer to the question "What Would Jesus Do?" is that when the time came to leave a tip, he would empty out his wallet, should the real Jesus have carried one.

The most dramatic attack on *Nickel and Dimed* occurred in 2003, when the University of North Carolina at Chapel Hill assigned the book to all incoming students. This prompted a group of conservative students and state legislators to hold a press conference denouncing *Nickel and Dimed* as a "classic Marxist rant" and a work of "intellectual pornography with no redeeming characteristics." The group proceeded to take out a full-page ad in the *Raleigh News & Observer,* which had little to say about the book, but charged me with being a Marxist, an atheist, and a dedicated enemy of the American family—this last proven by my longstanding conviction that families headed by single mothers are as deserving of support as those headed by married couples. I was greeted on North Carolina radio talk shows by hosts asking, "What does it feel like to be the antichrist of North Carolina?" and similarly challenging inquiries.

But while I was enjoying the free publicity, housekeepers on the UNC-CH campus put the brouhaha to good use by showing up at work wearing T-shirts and buttons reading, "Ask ME about being nickel and dimed." The housekeepers, it turned out, had been fighting for union recognition for years—against the very administration that had apparently approved *Nickel and Dimed* as freshman reading material. My involvement came to a glorious conclusion when the house-keepers and graduate student employees invited me to come to campus—on my own dime, of course—and speak at rallies for campus workers, although these unfortunately did not lead to union recognition.

But for the most part, the book has been far better received than I could have imagined it would be, with an impact extending well into the more comfortable classes. A Florida woman wrote to tell me that, before reading it, she'd always been annoyed at the poor for what she saw as their self-inflicted obesity. Now she understood that a healthy diet wasn't always an option. Another woman told me she'd always assumed that "unskilled" workers earned at least $15 an hour, which is what she paid her housekeeper. My sister in Colorado, who is by no means affluent herself, was so struck by the homeless workers I wrote about that she organized a local chapter of Habitat for Humanity. And if I had a quarter for every person who's told me he or she now tipped more generously, I would be able to start my own foundation.

What is even more gratifying to me is that the book has been widely read among low-wage workers themselves. In the last few years, hundreds of people have written to tell me their stories: the mother of a newborn infant whose electricity had just been turned off, the woman who had just been given a diagnosis of cancer and has no health insurance, the newly homeless man who writes from a library computer. To quote from a few of the e-mails I have received over the years:

Nickled and Dimed is far from fiction. It is pretty much my
life. With 2 college degrees, I have struggled, and with no
health insurance, I've incurred a ton of debt. I have not done
as well as my parents, who came out of the Depression. Our
government says there are jobs, but they are low-pay jobs
with no benefits. Not livable wage jobs. Not jobs that will
give you a house and savings for retirement. Nothing glim-
mers in this dust.

Hello, Barbara, I am a downsized federal employee, not white
collar, blue collar [whose] income was less than $20,000. . . .
After my 20 years in Data with the I.R.S. for $10.00 an hour,
$6000.00 in 401K I can't locate, I took a job as a Direct Care
Counselor, sort of like the nursing aide position you had in
Nickel & Dimed. Well I was hurt 4 months into this horri-
ble, physical degrading job basically cleaning up after Mentally Ill/Disabled population while doing a Take Down for
violent clients as we called them, and I messed up my knee,
three surgeries later needing knee replacement and out of
work for almost 5 years now I collect $65.75 a week from
worker's compensation insurance, from originally $256.00 a
week after surgery #1. Now I have to find a job that I can do
with a bad knee, because I can't survive any longer.

I just finished reading your book entitled "Nickel and
Dimed." I appreciate the fact that you were willing to experience first hand what many of us live with day to day. . . . You
witnessed the "pariah" syndrome the working poor experience daily. Very few people get the chance to delve into that
other realm where you feel like a lesser being just for being.

At the time I wrote *Nickel and Dimed,* I wasn't sure how many people it directly applied to—only that the official definition of poverty was way off the mark, since it defined an individual earning $7 an hour, as I did on average, as well out of poverty. But three months after the book was published, the Economic Policy Institute in Washington, D.C., issued a report entitled "Hardships in America: The Real Story of Working Families," which found an astounding 29 percent of American families living in what could be more reasonably defined as poverty, meaning that they earned less than a bare-bones budget covering housing, child care, health care, food, transportation, and taxes—though not, it should be noted, any entertainment, meals out, cable TV, Internet service, vacations, or holiday gifts. Twenty-nine percent is a minority, but not a reassuringly small one, and other studies in the early 2000s came up with similar figures.

The big question, ten years later, is whether things have improved or worsened for those in the bottom third of the income distribution, the people who clean hotel rooms, work in warehouses, wash dishes in restaurants, care for the very young and very old, and keep the shelves stocked in our stores. The short answer is that things have gotten much worse, especially since the economic downturn that began in 2008. When you read about the hardships I found people enduring while I was researching this book—the skipped meals, the lack of medical care, the occasional need to sleep in cars or vans—you should bear in mind that those occurred in the *best* of times. The economy was growing, and jobs, if poorly paid, were at least plentiful. In 2000, I had been able to walk into a number of jobs pretty much off the street. Less than a decade later, many of these jobs had disappeared and there was stiff competition for those that remained. It would have been impossible to repeat my *Nickel and Dimed* "experiment," had I had been so inclined, because I would probably never have found a job.

For the last couple of years, I have attempted to find out what was happening to the working poor in a declining economy—this time using conventional reporting techniques like interviewing. I started with my own extended family, which includes plenty of people without jobs or health insurance, and moved on to trying to track down a couple of the people I had met while working on *Nickel and Dimed*. This wasn't easy, because most of the addresses and phone numbers I had taken away with me had proved to be inoperative within a few months, probably due to moves and suspensions of telephone service. I had kept in touch with "Melissa" over the years, who was still working at Wal-Mart, where her wages had risen from $7 to $10 an hour, but in the meantime her husband had lost his job. "Caroline," now in her fifties and partly disabled by diabetes and heart disease, had left her deadbeat husband and was subsisting on occasional cleaning and catering jobs. Neither seemed unduly afflicted by the recession, but only because they had already been living in what amounts to a permanent economic depression.

Media attention has focused, understandably enough, on the "nouveau poor"—formerly middle and even upper-middle class people who lost their jobs, their homes, and/or their investments in the financial crisis and economic downturn that followed it, but the brunt of the recession has been borne by the blue-collar working class, which had already been sliding downwards since de-industrialization began in the 1980s. In 2008 and 2009, for example, blue-collar unemployment was increasing three times as fast as white-collar unemployment, and African American and Latino workers were three times as likely to be unemployed as white workers. Low-wage blue-collar workers, like the people I worked with in this book, were especially hard hit for the simple reason that they had so few assets and savings to fall back on as jobs disappeared.

How have the already-poor attempted to cope with their worsening economic situation? One obvious way is to cut back on health care. The *New York Times* reported in 2009 that one-third of Americans could no longer afford to comply with their prescriptions and that there had been a sizable drop in the use of medical care. Others, including members of my extended family, have given up their health insurance. Food is another expenditure that has proved vulnerable to hard times, with the rural poor turning increasingly to "food auctions," which offer items that may be past their sell-by dates. And for those who like their meat fresh, there's the option of urban hunting. In Racine, Wisconsin, a fifty-one-year old laid-off mechanic told me he was supplementing his diet by "shooting squirrels and rabbits and eating them stewed, baked, and grilled." In Detroit, where the wildlife population has mounted as the human population ebbs, a retired truck driver was doing a brisk business in raccoon carcasses, which he recommends marinating with vinegar and spices.

The most common coping strategy, though, is simply to increase the number of paying people per square foot of dwelling space—by doubling up or renting to couch-surfers. It's hard to get firm numbers on overcrowding, because no one likes to acknowledge it to census-takers, journalists, or anyone else who might be remotely connected to the authorities. In

Los Angeles, housing expert Peter Dreier says that "people who've lost their jobs, or at least their second jobs, cope by doubling or tripling up in overcrowded apartments, or by paying 50 or 60 or even 70 percent of their incomes in rent." According to a community organizer in Alexandria, Virginia, the standard apartment in a complex occupied largely by day laborers contains two bedrooms, each containing an entire family of up to five people, plus an additional person laying claim to the couch.

No one could call suicide a "coping strategy," but it is one way some people have responded to job loss and debt. There are no national statistics linking suicide to economic hard times, but the National Suicide Prevention Lifeline reported more than a four-fold increase in call volume between 2007 and 2009, and regions with particularly high unemployment, like Elkhart, Indiana, have seen troubling spikes in their suicide rates. Foreclosure is often the trigger for suicide—or, worse, murder-suicides that destroy entire families.

We do of course have a collective way of ameliorating the hardships of individuals and families—a government safety net that is meant to save the poor from spiraling down all the way to destitution. But its response to the economic emergency of the last few years has been spotty at best. The food-stamp program has responded to the crisis fairly well, to the point where it now reaches about 37 million people, up about 30 percent from pre-recession levels. But welfare—the traditional last resort for the down-and-out until it was "reformed" in 1996—only expanded by about 6 percent in the first two years of the recession. The difference between the two programs? There is a right to food stamps. You go to the office and, if you meet the statutory definition of need, they help you. For welfare, the street-level bureaucrats can, pretty much at their own discretion, just say no.

Take the case of Kristen and Joe Parente, Delaware residents who had always imagined that people turned to the government for help only if "they didn't want to work." Their troubles began well before the recession, when Joe, a fourth-generation pipe-fitter, sustained a back injury that left him unfit for even light lifting. He fell into a profound depression for several months, then rallied to ace a state-sponsored retraining course in computer repairs—only to find that those skills are no longer in demand. The obvious fallback was disability benefits, but—catch-22—when Joe applied he was told he could not qualify without presenting a recent MRI scan. This would cost $800–$900, which the Parentes do not have; nor has Joe, unlike the rest of the family, been able to qualify for Medicaid.

When they married as teenagers, the plan had been for Kristen to stay home with the children. But with Joe out of action and three children to support by the middle of this decade, Kristen went out and got waitressing jobs, ending up, in 2008, in a "pretty fancy place on the water." Then the recession struck and she was laid off. Kristen is bright, pretty, and to judge from her command of her own small kitchen, probably capable of holding down a dozen tables with precision and grace. In the past she'd always been able to land a new job within days; now there was nothing. Like 44 percent of laid-off people at the time, she failed to meet the fiendishly complex and sometimes arbitrary eligibility requirements for unemployment benefits. Their car started falling apart.

So the Parentes turned to what remains of welfare—TANF,

or Temporary Assistance to Needy Families. TANF does not offer straightforward cash support like Aid to Families with Dependent Children, which it replaced in 1996. It's an income supplementation program for working parents, and it was based on the sunny assumption that there would always be plenty of jobs for those enterprising enough to get them. After Kristen applied, nothing happened for six weeks—no money, no phone calls returned. At school, the Parentes' seven-year-old's class was asked to write out what wish they would present to a genie, should a genie appear. Brianna's wish was for her mother to find a job because there was nothing to eat in the house, an aspiration that her teacher deemed too disturbing to be posted on the wall with the other children's requests.

When the Parentes finally got into "the system" and began receiving food stamps and some cash assistance, they discovered why some recipients have taken to calling TANF "Torture and Abuse of Needy Families." From the start, the TANF experience was "humiliating," Kristen says. The caseworkers "treat you like a bum. They act like every dollar you get is coming out of their own paychecks." The Parentes discovered that they were each expected to apply for forty jobs a week, although their car was on its last legs and no money was offered for gas, tolls, or babysitting. In addition, Kristen had to drive thirty-five miles a day to attend "job readiness" classes offered by a private company called Arbor, which, she says, were "frankly a joke." Nationally, according to Kaaryn Gustafson of the University of Connecticut Law School, "applying for welfare is a lot like being booked by the police." There may be a mug shot, fingerprinting, and lengthy interrogations as to one's children's true paternity. The ostensible goal is to prevent welfare fraud, but the psychological impact is to turn poverty itself into a kind of crime.

The most shocking thing I learned from my research on the fate of the working poor in the recession was the extent to which poverty has indeed been criminalized in America. Perhaps the constant suspicions of drug use or threat that I encountered in low-wage workplaces should have alerted me to the fact that, when you leave the relative safety of the middle class, you might as well have given up your citizenship and taken residence in a hostile nation. Most cities, for example, have ordinances designed to drive the destitute off the streets by outlawing such necessary activities of daily life as sitting, loitering, sleeping, or lying down. Urban officials boast that there is nothing discriminatory about such laws: "If you're lying on a sidewalk, whether you're homeless or a millionaire, you're in violation of the ordinance," a St. Petersburg, Florida, city attorney stated in June 2009, echoing Anatole France's immortal observation that "the law, in its majestic equality, forbids the rich as well as the poor to sleep under bridges. . . ."

In defiance of all reason and compassion, the criminalization of poverty has actually intensified as the weakened economy generates ever more poverty. So concludes a recent study from the National Law Center on Poverty and Homelessness, which finds that the number of ordinances against the publicly poor has been rising since 2006, along with the harassment of the poor for more "neutral" infractions like jaywalking, littering, or carrying an open container. The report lists America's ten "meanest" cities—the largest of which include Los Angeles, Atlanta, and Orlando—but new contestants are springing up every day. In Colorado, Grand Junction's city council is considering a ban on begging; Tempe, Arizona, carried out a four-day crackdown on the indigent at the end of June. And how do you know when someone is indigent? As a Las Vegas statute puts it, "an indigent person is a person whom a reason-able ordinary person would believe to be entitled to apply for or receive" public assistance.

That could be me before the blow-drying and eyeliner, and it's definitely Al Szekeley at any time of day. A grizzled sixty-two-year-old, he inhabits a wheelchair and is often found on G Street in Washington, D.C.—the city that is ultimately responsible for the bullet he took in the spine in Fu-bai, Viet-nam, in 1972. He had been enjoying the luxury of an indoor bed until December 2008, when the police swept through the shelter in the middle of the night looking for men with outstanding warrants. It turned out that Szekeley, who is an ordained minister and does not drink, do drugs, or cuss in front of ladies, did indeed have one—for "criminal trespass-ing," as sleeping on the streets is sometimes defined by the law. So he was dragged out of the shelter and put in jail. "Can you imagine?" asked Eric Sheptock, the homeless advocate (himself a shelter resident) who introduced me to Szekeley. "They arrested a homeless man *in a shelter* for being home-less?"

The viciousness of the official animus toward the indigent can be breathtaking. A few years ago, a group called Food Not Bombs started handing out free vegan food to hungry people in public parks around the nation. A number of cities, led by Las Vegas, passed ordinances forbidding the sharing of food with the indigent in public places, leading to the arrests of sev-eral middle-aged white vegans. One anti-sharing law was just overturned in Orlando, but the war on illicit generosity con-tinues. Orlando is appealing the decision, and Middletown, Connecticut, is in the midst of a crackdown. More recently, Gainesville, Florida, began enforcing a rule limiting the number of meals that soup kitchens may serve to 130 people in one day, and Phoenix, Arizona, has been using zoning laws to stop a local church from serving breakfast to homeless people.

For the not-yet-homeless, there are two main paths to criminalization, and one is debt. Anyone can fall into debt, and although we pride ourselves on the abolition of debtors' prison, in at least one state, Texas, people who can't pay fines for things like expired inspection stickers may be made to "sit out their tickets" in jail. More commonly, the path to prison begins when one of your creditors has a court summons issued for you, which you fail to honor for one reason or another, such as that your address has changed and you never received it. Okay, now you're in "contempt of the court." Or suppose you miss a payment and your car insurance lapses, and then you're stopped for something like a broken headlight (about $130 for the bulb alone). Now, depending on the state, you may have your car impounded and/or face a steep fine— again, exposing you to a possible court summons. "There's just no end to it once the cycle starts," says Robert Solomon of Yale Law School. "It just keeps accelerating."

The second—and by far the most reliable—way to be criminalized by poverty is to have the wrong color skin. Indignation runs high when a celebrity professor succumbs to racial profiling, but whole communities are effectively "profiled" for the suspicious combination of being both dark skinned and poor. Flick a cigarette and you're "littering;" wear the wrong color T-shirt and you're displaying gang allegiance. Just strolling around in a dodgy neighborhood can mark you as a potential suspect. And don't get grumpy about it or you could be "resisting arrest."

In what has become a familiar pattern, the government defunds services that might help the poor while ramping up law enforcement: Shut down public housing, then make it a crime to be homeless. Generate no public-sector jobs, then penalize people for falling into debt. The experience of the poor, and especially poor people of color, comes to resemble that of a rat in a cage scrambling to avoid erratically administered electric shocks. And if you should try to escape this nightmare reality into a brief drug-induced high, it's "gotcha" all over again, because that of course is illegal too. One result is our staggering level of incarceration, the highest in the world; today exactly the same number of Americans—2.3 million— reside in prison as in public housing. And what public housing remains has become ever more prison-like, with random police sweeps and, in a growing number of cities, proposed drug tests for residents. The safety net, or what remains of it, has been transformed into a dragnet.

It is not clear whether economic hard times will finally force us to break the mad cycle of poverty and punishment. With even the official level of poverty increasing—to over 14 percent in 2010—some states are beginning to ease up on the criminalization of poverty—using alternative sentencing methods, shortening probation, and reducing the number of people locked up for technical violations like missing court appointments. But others, diabolically enough, are tightening the screws: not only increasing the number of "crimes," but charging prisoners for their room and board, guaranteeing they'll be released with potentially criminalizing levels of debt.

So what is the solution to the poverty of so many of America's working people? Ten years ago, when this book first came out, I often responded with the standard liberal wish list—a higher minimum wage, universal health care, affordable housing, good schools, reliable public transportation, and all the other things we, uniquely among the developed nations, have neglected to do.

Today the answer seems both more modest and more challenging: If we want to reduce poverty, we have to stop doing the things that make people poor and keep them that way. Stop underpaying people for the jobs they do. Stop treating working people as potential criminals and let them have the right to organize for better wages and working conditions. Stop the institutional harassment of those who turn to the government for help or find themselves destitute in the streets. Maybe, as so many Americans seem to believe today, we can't afford the kinds of public programs that would genuinely alleviate poverty—though I would argue otherwise. But at least we should decide, as a bare minimum principle, to stop kicking people when they're down.

acknowledgments

With thanks for all kinds of help to Michael Berman, Sara Bershtel, Chauna Brocht, Kristine Dahl, Tom Engelhardt, Frank Herd and Sarah Bourassa, Kristine Jacobs, Clara Jeffrey, Deb Konechne, Marc Linder, John Newton, Frances Fox Piven, Peter Rachleff, Bill Sokal, David Wagner, Jennifer Wheeler, and Patti.

a reader's guide

No matter which tax bracket you're in, you have a stake in the issues raised by Barbara Ehrenreich. A book that has changed assumptions about American prosperity and hardship, *Nickel and Dimed* makes an especially compelling selection for reading groups. The questions that follow are designed to enhance your personal understanding or group discussion of this provocative, heartfelt—and funny—account of life in the low-wage trenches.

questions for discussion

1. In the wake of recent welfare reform measures, millions of women entering the workforce can expect to face struggles like the ones Ehrenreich confronted in *Nickel and Dimed*.

Have you ever been homeless, unemployed, without health insurance, or held down two jobs? What is the lowest-paying job you ever held and what kind of help—if any—did you need to improve your situation?

2. Were your perceptions of blue-collar Americans transformed or reinforced by *Nickel and Dimed*? Have your notions of poverty and prosperity changed since reading the book? What about your own treatment of waiters, maids, and salespeople?

3. How do booming national and international chains—restaurants, hotels, retail outlets, cleaning services, and elder-care facilities—affect the treatment and aspirations of low-wage workers? Consider how market competition and the push for profits drive the nickel-and-diming of America's lowest-paid.

4. Housing costs pose the greatest obstacle for low-wage workers. Why does our society seem to resist rectifying this situation? Do you believe that there are realistic solutions to the lack of affordable housing?

5. While working for The Maids, Ehrenreich hears Ted claim that he's "not a bad guy . . . and cares a lot about his girls." How do the assumptions of supervisors such as Ted affect their employees? How does Ted compare to Ehrenreich's other bosses? To yours?

6. Ehrenreich is white and middle class. She asserts that her experience would have been radically different had she

been a person of color or a single parent. Do you think discrimination shaped Ehrenreich's story? In what ways?

7. Ehrenreich found that she could not survive on $7 per hour—not if she wanted to live indoors. Consider how her experiment would have played out in your community: limiting yourself to $7 per hour earnings, create a hypothetical monthly budget for your part of the country.

8. Ehrenreich experienced remarkable goodwill, generosity, and solidarity among her colleagues. Does this surprise you? How do you think your own colleagues measure up?

9. Why do you think low-wage workers are reluctant to form labor organizations, as Ehrenreich discovered at Wal-Mart? How do you think employees should lobby to improve working conditions?

10. Many campus and advocacy groups are currently involved in struggles for a "living wage." How do you think a living wage should be calculated?

11. Were you surprised by the casual reactions of Ehrenreich's coworkers when she revealed herself as an undercover writer? Were you surprised that she wasn't suspected of being "different" or out-of-place despite her graduate-level education and usually comfortable lifestyle?

12. How does managers' scrutiny—"time theft" crackdowns and drug testing—affect workers' morale? How can American companies make the workplace environment

safe and efficient without treating employees like suspected criminals?

13. Ehrenreich concluded that had her working life been spent in a Wal-Mart–like environment, she would have emerged a different person—meaner, pettier, "Barb" instead of "Barbara." How would your personality change if you were placed in working conditions very different from the ones you are in now?

14. The workers in *Nickel and Dimed* receive almost no benefits—no overtime pay, no retirement funds, and no health insurance. Is this fair? Do you think an increase in salary would redress the lack of benefits, or is this a completely separate problem?

15. Many of Ehrenreich's colleagues relied heavily on family— for housing and help with child-care, by sharing appliances and dividing up the cooking, shopping, and cleaning. Do you think Americans make excessive demands on the family unit rather than calling for the government to help those in need?

16. *Nickel and Dimed* takes place in 1998–2000, a time of unprecedented prosperity in America. Do you think Ehrenreich's experience would be different in today's economy? How so?

17. After reading *Nickel and Dimed,* do you think that having a job—any job—is better than no job at all? Did this book make you feel angry? Better informed? Relieved that someone has finally described your experience? Galvanized to do something?